SPIRITUAL AUTHORITY
FUNDAMENTALS

VICTORY FOR EVERYDAY LIVING

IFEOMA OKECHUKWU

PROFESSIONAL PUBLISHING MEETS POWERFUL PROMOTION

A wholly owned subsidiary of **TBN**

Spiritual Authority Fundamentals

Trilogy Christian Publishers A Wholly Owned Subsidiary of Trinity Broadcasting Network

2442 Michelle Drive Tustin, CA 92780

Manufactured in the United States of America

10 9 8 7 6 5 4 3 2 1

Library of Congress Cataloging-in-Publication Data is available.

ISBN: 978-1-63769-450-3

E-ISBN: 978-1-63769-451-0

FOREWORD

According to Proverbs 4:7 wisdom is the principal thing; Therefore, get wisdom. And in all your getting, get understanding. (NKJV)

Everyone needs practical instruction, wisdom and understanding in how to apply biblical truths to see the results that Jesus promised to His disciples. Spiritual authority is one of those topics in the arena of grace and faith that manyseem to not understand or operate in. There is so much more in addition to just getting born again and hanging on until reaching heaven. We are called to live in victory, not defeat!

Every born again, Spirit filled believer has been equipped with power and authority but most haven't gained the instruction or understanding of the practical application in overcoming and seeing victory over sickness, disease or demonic oppression.

This book is really a handbook of the practical principals based solidly on the Word of God in applying faith with grace and seeing supernatural results.

I have known Ifeoma as a dear sister for several years, She has attended our church and is one of our Grace Life

Instructors who teaches classes regularly and serves as a prayer minister to those in need of a dose of the power of God to work in their lives.

Ifeoma also has her own missions ministry and she evangelizes and preaches by radio and in person to different audiences in Nigeria for several months during the year.

Her experience and biblical knowledge has been a tremendous blessing in setting people free from all kinds of sickness and disease in Nigeria and this House!

In her book, Ifeoma gets right down to business in the teaching and application with real life experiences and demonstrates the "how to's" of wielding the Spiritual Authority given to each of us.

I heartily recommend this book and pray that as you read this, the impact in your mind and heart will inspire faith and confidence in the Word of God and who He is

in you as you take your Spiritual Authority over "all the power of the enemy" and see great victories from now on.

Mike Gonyer – Pastor, House On The Rock Church, Ypsilanti Michigan

ACKNOWLEDGMENTS

I want to specially acknowledge the help of all the people involved in the success story of this book, specifically, the editors, reviewers, illustrators, and those who offered valuable encouragement during the review process. Their support has made this book a reality.

First, I would like to thank Carol Angel Sharp and Hope Adah, the first reviewers of the book, for their contributions at the beginning stages of the book. My sincere gratitude also goes to Meg Obiomah, the main editor, for her diligence, insightful suggestions and professionalism in the editing and the presentation of the chapters. I owe a great indebtedness to Dan Den Houter, a retired writer, who thoroughly combed through the first edition of the book. I'm grateful for his time and expertise, in giving valuable editing suggestions for the second edition of the book. I am very grateful to Dee Farrel Emrick and Haley Jula, a mother and daughter team, for their hard work in editing suggestions and designing the inside and the cover of the first edition of this book.

Second, I wish to acknowledge the valuable contributions of my Pastor, Mike Goyner, who also wrote the Foreword of this book.

Most of all, I want to acknowledge my husband, Jude Okechukwu, for his moral support and assistance in helping me choose the cover of the book, and my sons Michael and Chukwudi Okechukwu for proof-reading some aspect of the book, and my daughter, Favor Okechukwu, for her technical assistance in the graphics in the book.Spiritual Authority Fundamentals: Victory for Everyday Living could not have been a success without the help of everyone mentioned here.

TABLE OF CONTENTS

PREFACE

This is the first book of the *For Believers Only* series, which details the realities of the Christian faith. *Spiritual Authority Fundamentals: Victory For Everyday Living* addresses a specific spiritual reality for born-again Christians, to aid them in their search on how best to maintain the victory CHRIST won for them.

With the many lessons learned from my walk with GOD, I felt led to publish *Spiritual Authority Fundamentals: Victory For Everyday Living* first, not necessarily because it was the first to be completed, but because there seems to be a gap between what's available under this topic and where many Christians are in their understanding of a believer's spiritual realities; hence the urgency to complete and publish this book.

Many people address me as an evangelist because I have dedicated almost half of my born-again life to sharing the Gospel, mostly with unbelievers. However, I recall that many times within the last decade, I have found myself crying passionately for my fellow believers, who seem to have only a limited understanding of what Christianity is all about. Many believers only understand the final destination for salvation (eternity in Heaven); and few know and experience our spiritual reality that enhances our earthly transition to that final destination.

Therefore, *Spiritual Authority Fundamentals* exists to provide additional insight into the spiritual components of a born-again Christian and expound on why our GOD-given spiritual authority is critical in maintaining the victory JESUS paid such a huge price to give to us.

One distinct feature of my books, including this one, is my sense of the inadequacy of writing GOD's names in the same letter case you'd typically expect. So, the names GOD, FATHER, JESUS CHRIST, HOLY SPIRIT, and HOLY GHOST are all capitalized. I hope that this rather unorthodox way of honoring GOD would not bother readers. In the same vein, satan has been given his place, with his name beginning with the lower case.

Most biblical references in this book are from the King James Version, but occasionally, I have used and referenced other translations.

If this book has helped you gain an increased understanding of the spiritual authority that you have, why it is necessary to have it, and how to exercise it, then recommend *Spiritual Authority Fundamentals: Victory For Everyday Living* to a brother or sister in CHRIST.

Seeking GOD, finding HIM, and discovering the ever-increasing love and magnanimity of GOD, leaves me in deeper awe of HIM. I hope you can say the same; if not now, then at a certain point in your journey with HIM.

Ifeoma Okechukwu, Ph. D.

Favoured Beulah International

Farmington Hills, Michigan

August 2020

INTRODUCTION

The subject of Spiritual Authority is a vast, all-encompassing area. Indeed, in all of Christian doctrine, the whole discourse of our spiritual authority in CHRIST cannot be easily exhausted in one book. This concept is so important that every Christian should understand and exercise it. Many Christians usually understand the term, Spiritual Authority, to mean casting out of devils; while in actual fact, it includes authority over all devils, as well as enforcing obedience to the word of GOD on circumstances, situations and all other activities of demonic spirits which are subject to the believer.

It is my earnest desire, in this book, to delve into these areas, working on their inter-relationships, and show how every Christian should live in this reality. These same spiritual principles that affect our personal lives, when scaled up, would also affect an entire church and even whole nations.

JESUS CHRIST gave HIS disciples, the first people who believed in HIM, authority to preach the gospel, to heal sicknesses and diseases, and to cast out devils (Matthew 10:1, 8; Luke 9:1). Furthermore, other Bible passages show that the authority and power to heal the sick and cast out devils automatically follows anyone who believes in JESUS CHRIST (Mark 16:15-18, Ephesians 1:19).

Although some believers argue that this authority and power are not for us today, those who believe otherwise continue to manifest healing and power over satan in their lives, ministries, and in the lives of others, including notable ministers like Curry Blake, Andrew Wommack, Kenneth Copeland, David Hogan, Bishop Keith A. Butler, and among the deceased: Kenneth Hagin, A.A. Allen, Reinhard Bonnke, Smith Wigglesworth and John G. Lake, just to mention a few. The gifts of GOD are without repentance (Romans 11:29), but whether or not a believer manifests them depends on his level of faith (Matthew 8:13; 9:29-30; 15:8). Because of the gift of freewill, no one manifests any work of righteousness they do not believe (Mark 9:23; Luke 1:45; John 11:40). If you believe, you too will manifest the authority and power of GOD.

> **Because of the gift of freewill, no one manifests any work of righteousness they do not believe. If you believe, you too will manifest the authority and power of GOD.**

Matthew 8:13 (KJV)

*"And Jesus said unto the centurion, 'Go thy way; and **as thou hast believed, [so] be it done unto thee.**' And his servant was healed in the selfsame hour"* (emphasis is mine).

14

Introduction

Some claim that the instructions of Mark 16:17-18 were not included in the oldest manuscripts, but CHRIST gave similar instructions to the disciples. Many of those Christians pray "The Lord's Prayer" that JESUS taught the disciples, because they believe that it applies to all believers, but then they give excuses about HIS instructions concerning healings and casting out devils. Because of the GOD-given free will of man, no one can experience anything beyond what they believe, and therefore, all who do not believe the authority and power given to believers will not experience them.

> **All who do not believe the authority and power given to believers will not experience them.**

Mark 16:17-18 (KJV)

*"And **these signs shall follow them that believe**; In my name shall they cast out devils; they shall speak with new tongues; 18 They shall take up serpents; and if they drink any deadly thing, it shall not hurt them; they shall lay hands on the sick, and they shall recover" (Emphasis mine).*

The acts of picking up venomous serpents and drinking deadly things are physical and metaphorical, but the authority given to believers in this passage is spiritual. Also, speaking in new tongues (that are not learned, and mostly not understood by human beings, including the speaker), casting out devils, safety from picking up serpents and drinking of deadly things, and healing the sick by the laying of hands, are all supernatural phenomena. The power of GOD is guaranteed in this passage for the safety of the believer.

Carnal believers, (meaning believers who operate mostly from the humanistic perspective) cannot experience the victorious life promised in this passage, over their circumstances, situations, and the devil's activities against them. However, if you accept these truths today and believe that JESUS is speaking to you in this passage, then you too will do "greater works" (John 14:12) than JESUS did during HIS earthly ministry, because "JESUS CHRIST (is still) the same yesterday, and today, and forever" (Hebrews 13:8). The authority and power described in these passages of the Bible are given to all believers, including you. It is not just for the pastors and other ministers of GOD; they are for you as well. The truth is that the ministers are given to the church to enable all the "Janes and John Does" of the church to exhibit the power and glory of GOD, by being always ready to exercise their authority to do HIS work (Ephesians 4:11-12).

Ephesians 4:11-12 (NLT)

11 "Now these are the gifts Christ gave to the church: the apostles, the prophets, the evangelists, and the pastors and teachers.

12 Their responsibility is to equip God's people to do his work and build up the church, the body of Christ."

Authority is delegated power to act on behalf of another. Therefore, the authority that Christians utilize to enforce obedience through the word of GOD on their circumstances, situations, and demonic spirits (like foul spirits and spirits of infirmity) is CHRIST's. Any attempt to exercise the authority and power otherwise, will fail! Because

Spiritual authority is the power of attorney to act on GOD's behalf.

of the sacrificial work of JESUS, we as Christians, have the power of attorney to act on HIS behalf (John 14:12-14)! Praise the LORD!

Although this book is not focused on the casting out of devils or exorcism, that is prevalent in many churches and deliverance ministries, it still presents a limited highlight about overcoming demonic activities. Deliverance from demonic operations are not supposed to be the focus of any ministry, neither should any ministry focus exclusively on speaking in tongues or healing the sick, picking up serpents, drinking of deadly things, etc., thus elevating them above the preaching the gospel. These signs and wonders follow the preaching of the gospel, not the other way round.

These fundamental principles are laid out in ten chapters that constitute a solid foundation for the believer's authority and highlight the superiority of the power of living in the spirit (in accordance with the Spirit and the Word of GOD) rather than in the flesh (in accordance with natural, human desires).

CHAPTER ONE
UNDERSTANDING SPIRITUAL AUTHORITY

If you are a new believer, recently born into the Kingdom of GOD (according to Romans 10:9) you need to understand the rights, privileges and opportunities that are available to you, as well as the associated responsibilities, which would enable you to operate more effectively in your new abode.

Spiritual authority is the second most essential privilege or right that you receive from GOD through our LORD JESUS CHRIST, with the first as your new birth. Knowledge of this helps you access and function in all the other blessings and gifts of GOD in CHRIST. In this book, you will get to learn these fundamental truths, and have a solid foundation for other doctrinal truths.

Definition of Spiritual Authority

A look at a few definitions of Spiritual Authority would help, at this time, to set the records straight. It would also serve as a rallying point for subsequent discussions on our topic.

Spiritual authority is defined, at this point, as "the right or privilege given by GOD through our LORD JE-SUS CHRIST to enforce obedience to the word of GOD, on circumstances, situations and every spirit that is subject to believers" (Okechukwu, 2020d).

This definition of spiritual authority and its accompanying implications, which were developed over many years of my experience with the word of GOD, will be explained and used throughout this book.

Another interesting definition goes thus: "Divinely authorized rights and responsibilities delegated to Christians to act on GOD's behalf in spiritually ruling over HIS creation, under the LORDSHIP of JESUS CHRIST" (Dr. Tony Evans).

The Importance of Spiritual Authority

A believer's spiritual authority is the second most important gift of GOD, with the first being the gift of the new birth in CHRIST that enhances a believer's ability to effectively manifest the power of GOD and works of righteousness on earth. Your spiritual authority in CHRIST is important for several reasons. First of all, you have to understand that you are a spirit. Therefore, GOD relates with you as such. Everything you receive from GOD, is first spiritual, then natural, to fit our earth realm. The following are a few examples of your spiritual realities that you need to acquaint yourself with:

- All that pertains to life and godliness (2 Peter 1:3)

- All your blessings in heavenly places (Ephesians 1:3)

- All power and authority given to the believer (Luke 10:19; Mark 16:17-18)

- The anointing which you received when you believed (1 John 2:27)

- The same quality and quantity of faith as the apostles had (2 Peter 1:1)

First of all, you have to understand that you are a spirit. Therefore, GOD relates with you as such. Everything you receive from GOD, is first spiritual, then natural, to fit our earth realm.

To effectively manifest these graces, you have to exercise your spiritual authority. For example, the truth is that CHRIST has fully paid for your good health and healing but if you get sick, you would need to exercise your authority by speaking your healing for yourself or stand in agreement with another Christian to exercise your authority over any sickness or disease (Mark 16:18).

Another major truth you must understand is that GOD is a Spirit (John 4:24). HE lives in the realm of the spirit and everything HE does, manifests as spiritual reality first, before showing up in the physical, natural realm. An example is the creation of man. Let's consider this:

First, GOD created man.

Genesis 1:26 has a spiritual model of the man GOD made; then in Chapter Two, HE actually formed the man with dirt (Genesis 2:7).

> *Genesis 1:27 (NKJV)*
>
> *"**God created man** in HIS [own] image; in the image of GOD HE created him; male and female HE created them."*

Secondly, HE formed the man HE had created:

> *Genesis 2:7 (NKJV)*
>
> *"And **the LORD God formed man [of] the dust of the ground,** and breathed into his nostrils the **breath of life**; and man became a living being."*

Understanding the fundamentals of spiritual authority is important for all born again Christians, for several reasons. Firstly, there are some backslidden Christians who feel that they didn't succeed in their lives as Christians because Christianity failed in fulfilling its promises to them, especially in meeting their personal needs. If they had understood the basic principles of spiritual authority, they would have known how to overcome such issues. Let me illustrate this.

I met a certain lady in church and we became friends. She became frustrated about her life and called me to complain thus: "Someone from work told me that Christianity would help me find solutions to some of my problems, including getting married; and they encouraged me to join a church, which I did. But Minister Ifeoma, it is not working for me." Linda said. (Linda is not her real name).

I went ahead and asked her about how she was living her life before joining our church, and she explained that she was "living big" and "had been bad." The several attempts I made to help her to gain a different perspective on her situation were not very successful. Then, I realized that my friend was angry at GOD, which is exactly what the enemy wanted.

The Bible gives us an indication of this in the story of Job. Job's wife is an example of how the ultimate desire of satan, is for a believer to "curse GOD and die" (Job 2:9). The enemy would convince a Christian that their situation is so bad that they were better off dead than alive. Sometimes, depending on their orientation, or the church they be-

> **The enemy would convince a Christian that their situation is so bad that they were better off dead than alive.**

longed to, blaming and cursing GOD for their situation can very quickly become appealing to them.

In my experience, I have noticed that some people who call themselves atheists, arrived at their present state by blaming GOD for their unfulfilled dreams and tragedies. A name that quickly comes to mind is Dan Barker, a famous musician, who asked the question, "How happy can you be when you think every action and thought is being monitored by a judgmental ghost?" He said this while affirming rationalism as the guaranteed path to a happy existence. His question affirms that his problem was not about the existence of GOD, but Dan's understanding of the true nature of GOD, and his lack of knowledge about the rights and privileges that he had as a believer.

Secondly, there are other backslidden Christians (1 John 2:19), who have left the faith, not because GOD disappointed them, but because they were never committed to HIM in the first place. The Spirit of GOD, through John, said:

1 John 2:19 (NKJV)

"They went out from us, but they were not of us; for if they had been of us, they would have continued with us; but [they went out] that they might be made manifest, that none of them were of us."

The above quotation from John, the Apostle, could

come across as a circular argument, but it is a clear representation of the realities of the lack of knowledge, understanding and the belief system of many who sit on the pews of many churches today. A great number of people in the churches identify themselves as Christians for various reasons, but they may not be true believers. I have had encounters with many of them in my over fifteen years of mission trips, to a couple of African countries, but mostly in Nigeria.

Being a former atheist, I often sympathize with, and feel that I understand atheists; thus, I have been able to help many come to terms with what their real issues were, and these issues vary. I am not always inclined to give the testimony of my journey from atheism to theism but each time I do, I am amazed at the number of people who would speak with me in private to affirm that while I was speaking, I touched some nerves in their belief systems.

A branch pastor of one of the popular denominations in Nigeria was one of such people. This pastor had graduated from the university and could not find a job, so he applied to be considered to lead a branch of this popular denomination. He was hired, trained and soon after, he became a pastor. In January 2008, he participated in one of our open-air meetings where, during my sermon, I gave the testimony of how I became born again. When the invitation was made for those who wanted prayers, he was one of the people who responded.

I personally talked and prayed with him. He had been a pastor for about five years. At that point in time, he neither believed the stories in the Bible nor the existence of a supreme GOD. The good news was that he got converted and he is still growing strong in the LORD the last time I checked.

There are also similar situations in the United States, where some ministers do not actually believe in the existence of GOD, but keep on as Ministers of GOD because of the fear of losing their pay checks. The ones who do not believe and acknowledge it seem preferred by GOD (Revelation 3:15-16).

Thirdly, there are those that I refer to as "unbelieving believers," that is, they wear the cloak of Christianity but in actual fact, do not believe. There are two types of "unbelieving believers:" first, Christians who are convinced and believe in the existence of GOD but sometimes have difficulty or fail to demonstrate their faith or manifest GOD's blessings, gifts and promises (Mark 9:24).

> *Mark 9:24 (KJV) says:*
>
> *"And straightway the father of the child cried out, and said with tears, Lord, I believe; help thou mine unbelief."*

The second type of the "unbelieving believers" are

convinced that they do not believe. They really don't care whether GOD exists or not, but they stay in church for whatever reason, and keep looking out for the slightest excuse to leave (1 John 2:9). Some in this category confess that they believe but their lifestyle and character demonstrate that they do not (Titus 1:16).

As Titus 1:16 (KJV) says:

"They profess that they know God; but in works they deny [him], being abominable, and disobedient, and unto every good work reprobate."

Some open atheists could be more easily recognized than the second type of "unbelieving believers." Pope Benedict XVI (Vatican City, Nov 14, 2012 /10:45 am) referred to the second group of unbelievers as "practical atheists," meaning professing Christians who practice atheism in all they do. According to the Pope, practical atheists "say they are Christian, but live as if God does not exist." According to him, they constitute "a greater threat" than actual atheists do.

The way I see it, the lack of adequate teaching in the church and the misunderstanding of sound doctrine could be responsible for people leaving the faith and becoming open atheists or in-church "practical atheists." The outcome for both is usually the same: they do not manifest or enjoy any of GOD's blessings that they desire; subsequently, they walk away from the church, claiming that Christianity does not or did not work for them. Meanwhile, they car-

They do not believe, they don't exercise and cannot manifest their spiritual authority., ry in them the basic raw materials which they could have used to produce what they needed (which GOD had already provided) but because they do not believe, they don't exercise and cannot manifest their spiritual authority, in order to access and to birth what they need in their lives.

Going back to our model from Genesis, we see that GOD created a garden with all kinds of plants, animals, and perfect cosmic conditions for the increase and multiplication of things. He also endowed the man HE had made with the ability to prosper in the earth. The ability to prosper is the first indication of what is generally known as "blessing."

Genesis 1:22 (NKJV)

*"And **God blessed them**, saying, 'Be fruitful and multiply, and fill the waters in the seas, and let birds multiply on the earth.'"*

Genesis 1:28 (NKJV)

*"Then **God blessed them, and God said to them, 'Be fruitful and multiply**; fill the earth and subdue it; have dominion over the fish of the sea, over the birds of the air, and over every living thing that moves on the earth.'"*

Genesis 9:1 (NKJV)

*"So, **God blessed Noah and his sons, and said to them: 'Be fruitful and multiply,** and fill the earth.'"*

Notice that in Genesis 1:22, 28 above, GOD blessed them, saying, "Be fruitful and multiply," and replenish or populate the earth. The three verses referenced above, contain the key scriptures which establish the first use of and therefore, the meaning of the word "blessed:" a pronouncement of GOD to a living thing to prosper, which causes that living thing to possess the pronounced abilities or blessing.

Also, note that at the creation, GOD did not say that HE would continue to create new living things; rather, HE created them with seeds within them to reproduce after their own kind. Thus, Genesis 1:11, 12, 21, 24 and 25, activated the processes of reproduction when GOD blessed them. In other words, this was a two-step process of making sure that living things possessed the technical features for reproduction and increase; then GOD provided the Spirit that would always be present to activate the process (John 6:63). In this scripture, we see that the Word of GOD is life giving; it

GOD blessed them, saying, "Be fruitful and multiply,"

creates, activates, animates, and causes everything to work prosperously as intended.

John 6:63 (KJV)

It is the spirit that quickeneth; the flesh profiteth nothing: **the words that I speak unto you, [they] are spirit, and [they] are life**.

GOD also blessed the seventh day, the day after all creation (Genesis 2:3). Although the seventh day was not created after the pattern of the other creatures, yet the blessing produced on the seventh day can be seen to follow the same pattern of prosperity when one reviews the lives of those who observed the Sabbath, (the name given to the seventh day in Exodus 16). Genesis 2:3 did not include the invocation of the "increase and multiply" but it stated why GOD blessed the day after HE had completed creation. HE blessed that day as the Sabbath day because HE joyfully rested after the accomplishment of the completion of the creation of ALL that man needed to "dress and keep" the earth.

To dress and keep the earth means to work, serve, execute and be a husbandman (*Strong's Concordance*). These were the first instructions man received. As part of the law given to man because of increased wickedness and the evil of his heart, GOD added an instruction to rest on the Sabbath day: a requirement to remind man that GOD is the source of his blessings (Deuteronomy 5:15). This is why it is important to recognize that the Sabbath day rest of GOD was instituted before the fall of man and before the law was given to Moses; therefore, it is of great significance in man's relationship with GOD. The Sabbath day, being the seventh day, the day after creation, was when GOD rested – not from being fatigued – but with what should seem like a sense of accomplishment. He rested from the completion of creation.

Genesis 2:3 (NKJV)

"Then God blessed the seventh day and sanctified it, because in it He rested from all His work which God had created and made."

The garden, the first abode of man after creation, was called Eden, which means "pleasure" (*Strong's Concordance*). This connotes peace and restfulness. The word "Sabbath" was not used until hundreds of years later when GOD rescued the Israelites from the bondage in Egypt. HE instructed them to rest on the seventh day of the week and made the sixth day a day of the double-portion. The Israelites were instructed to gather a double portion of their normal ration of manna on the sixth day, for use on the seventh day, as they would not find any manna on that day, because GOD wanted them to rest on the seventh day. Although the Israelites did not work on the Sabbath day, they always had plenty to sustain them on that special day of rest (Exodus 16:5-30).

In his December 13th 2011 article in *The True Meaning of The Sabbath, (One Year with JESUS Devotional),* Andrew Wommack briefly explained the reason for the commandment of the Sabbath day rest for the Jews, as follows:

"The Sabbath was first mentioned in scripture in Exodus 16, when the LORD miraculously provided manna to the children of Israel in the wilderness. The Israelites were commanded to gather twice as much manna on the sixth day because God would not provide any on the seventh day" (Ex. 16:5, 22-30).

Shortly after this, the LORD commanded the observance of the Sabbath day in the Ten Commandments (written on two tablets of stone) that were given to Moses, which he received on Mt. Sinai (Ex. 20:8-11). In this command, GOD connected the Sabbath day with the rest HE took on the seventh day of creation.

In the book of Leviticus, the law concerning the Sabbath day rest became a means used by GOD, to develop in the Israelites an accurate mindset and attitude towards GOD, seeing HIM as the owner of all things, and them as stewards.

Leviticus 25:21-22 (NKJV)

"Then I will command My blessing on you in the sixth year, and it will bring forth produce enough for three years. [22] And you shall sow in the eighth year, and eat old produce until the

ninth year; until its produce comes in, you shall eat of the old harvest."

The law of the Sabbath day rest required them to have the mindset of stewards, who were living in obedience and commitment to God, and working hard to increase the value of what God entrusted to their care. The guaranteed outcome was a three-fold harvest of blessing in one year, as they allowed the farmland to be replenished (during the fallow period). This helped to restore its fertility for continued productivity within the next six years.

According to Exodus 23:12, one of the purposes of the Sabbath, was to give to man and his animals, one day of physical rest, each week. Today's medical science has proven that for us to function at our peak, our bodies need at least one day of rest each week. Deuteronomy 5:15 also clearly states that the Sabbath was to serve as a reminder to the Jews that they had been slaves in Egypt and were delivered from bondage, not by their own efforts but by the supernatural power of GOD.

Again, Wommack also states the significance of the Sabbath for the New Testament believers, which is entering into GOD's rest, as a show of ultimate intimacy with HIM (Hebrews 4:11).

In conclusion, GOD, who created the human body,

knew that one day out of every seven days, would be needed for the body to rest and replenish, physically, mentally and spiritually (Exodus 23:12). Human beings are generally known to be more productive and energized after one day of rest (from six days of hard labor). Therefore, the day of rest, is a day that is blessed, to prosper the children of GOD.

As we have seen from all the scriptures above, GOD endowed man with the ability to increase and multiply. Since you know that you have the active ingredients in you for your prosperity, you should look more on the inside of you for the manifestations of your blessings, rather than think that GOD is somehow responsible for keeping them from you. You are endowed with the authority to bring forth to the physical what GOD HAS ALREADY GIVEN YOU! It is part of exercising your spiritual authority. Realize that your blessings are in the spiritual realities and need to be transformed into the physical, in material terms. Moreover, you have the GOD-given authority to access the spiritual realm at will, in order to enforce the release of any of your gifts that are delaying to show up. Praise the LORD!

Implications of our spiritual authority

1. With every authority is an associated responsibility. Christians are comparable to law enforcement agents operating in the kingdom of GOD, because

we are enforcing the word of GOD. (Philemon 1:6, Mark 16:16-18; Matthew 10:8; Romans 8:19). Thus, you are a GOD's Word Enforcement Agent!

2. Every circumstance, situation and activity of spirits can be changed to the obedience of the word of GOD (Mark 11:22-24).

Thus, you are a GOD's Word Enforcement Agent!

3. An authority is as powerful as the force behind it. The value of an authority depends on the power behind it; thus the believer's authority is not insubstantial. No human or spirit can override the believer's authority because it is given by GOD. (Matthew 10:1, 28:18-20; Mark 16:15-18; Luke 9:1, 10:1, 19; John 14:12-14)

4. Spiritual Authority is an integral part of who a believer is (John 1:12-13; Ephesians 1).

5. Spiritual authority is not assigned differently but specially, by virtue of you being born again into the household of GOD. It is not what you do, but who you are (Mark 16:17a). It is the chief of the signs that follow after your "yes" to JESUS CHRIST! **You don't fast and pray for it; it's yours from your new birth!**

All you need to start walking in victory is acknowledging that you have the spiritual authority.

All you need to start walking in victory is acknowledging that you have the spiritual authority; then, when you make up your mind to exercise that authority, anything, circumstance, situation or spirit would submit to GOD's power that resides in you. So rise to your feet, or get into your closet; speak and expect something to happen and you will see results.

Historical background of our Spiritual Authority

From the beginning, at the creation of man, GOD's desire was for man to rule over HIS creation.

Genesis 1: 26

*"Then God said, 'Let us make man in our image, according to our likeness, let him have **dominion** over the fish of the sea, over the birds of the air and over the cattle of the field, over all the earth and over all creeping thing that creeps on the earth.'"*

Dominion according to *Strong's Definitions*:

The Hebrew word רָדָה râdâh, raw-daw'; a primitive

root; means to tread down, i.e. subjugate; specifically, to crumble off: — (come to, make to) have dominion, prevail against, reign, (bear, make to) rule, (-r, over), take.

GOD gave man dominion, that is, authority over all created things, as well as empowering the man HE made to name the animals (Genesis 2:19). GOD at the beginning gave man authority over all the works of HIS hands. Adam and Eve gave that authority to satan when they conceded to eat the forbidden fruit (Romans 6:16).

Romans 6:16 says that you are the servant of whoever you choose to obey. Adam and Eve choose to obey the devil and therefore yielded their authority to him. We know that satan took possession of Adam's earth by simply getting Adam to unwittingly hand it over to him by disobeying GOD. According to Luke:

Luke 4:6-8 (KJV)

6 "And the devil said unto him, 'All this power [meaning authority] will I give thee, and the glory of them: for that is delivered unto me; and to whomsoever I will I give it. 7 If thou therefore wilt worship me, all shall be thine.'

8 And Jesus answered and said unto him, 'Get thee behind me, satan: for it is written, "Thou shalt worship the LORD thy God, and him only shalt thou serve."

While tempting JESUS to bow down and worship him, satan implied that he had received the authority over all the kingdoms of the earth. JESUS did not yield to satan, neither did HE refute the latter's claim about his authority over the earth. However, the good news is that through our LORD JESUS CHRIST, the authority was restored to the born-again Christian – the new man in CHRIST.

The definition of spiritual authority we have developed suggests that as a born again Christian, you have authority over everything and over all spirits except GOD. GOD is a Spirit (John 4:24), but HE IS NOT SUBJECT TO BELIEVERS.

Believers have authority over everything through the name of JESUS, but many don't exercise it because they are not always mindful of who they are and their position in CHRIST. Since they are not conscious of it, they will not exercise it, and if they don't exercise their spiritual authority they will not manifest the anticipated result. However, by reading through this book, every sincere learner will be positioned, instructed and educated in their rights and authority in CHRIST, as well as how to use them effectively.

CHAPTER TWO
A DIVINE PRIVILEGE

From our earlier discourse, we saw that GOD gave man authority, as recorded in the Old, as well as the New Testaments. As we mentioned in the introduction, the dominion or authority to rule over GOD's creation was the first blessing HE pronounced upon man. We saw that in the Old Testament, man was given dominion over all the creation of GOD. In the New Testament, Christians are given authority and associated power to act on behalf of GOD (John 20:21-23; Matthew 18:18).

John 20:21-23 (NKJV)

21 "So Jesus said to them again, 'Peace to you! As the Father has sent Me, I also send you.'

22 And when He had said this, He breathed on [them,] and said to them, 'Receive the Holy Spirit.

23 If you forgive the sins of any, they are forgiven them; if you retain the [sins] of any, they are retained.'"

Matthew 18:18 (NKJV)

"Assuredly, I say to you, whatever you bind on earth will be bound in heaven, and whatever you loose on earth will be loosed in heaven."

When satan and his cohorts are bound and their activities stopped or changed, heaven honors and confirms it. JESUS gave HIS disciples and new converts authority, and emphasized in Luke 10:18 that HE had seen satan fall from his glory; therefore, the disciples had authority and power over him (Matthew 10:1, 8; Luke 9:1, 10:1, 19; Mark 16:15-18; Colossians 2:15). Hence as a believer:

> **When satan and his cohorts are bound and their activities stopped or changed, heaven honors and confirms it.**

1. You have authority as a son of GOD (John 1:12)

2. You have authority and power over ALL devils. (Luke 9:1) and over ALL the power of the enemy (Luke 10:19; Mark 16:17)

3. You have authority over angels (Hebrews 1:13-14).

Every believer in CHRIST JESUS is already blessed, according to Ephesians 1:3. The blessing has already been released and is not something that is yet to happen. Some preachers erroneously teach that the blessings that GOD has given believers are futuristic: something yet to be given or yet to occur; but this is as further from the truth as can be.

The truth is that JESUS fully paid for our sin by HIS death on the cross and thus qualified believers to become sons of GOD. JESUS redeemed us from all curses that could possibly be against us and hence released to us the blessings that had been held up from us (Galatians 3:13; Colossians 2:14-15). Similarly, because we are sons, we have been "blessed with all spiritual blessings in heavenly places in CHRIST" (Ephesians 1:3) and the first on the list of our blessings is our spiritual authority (Genesis 1:26-28).

Every blessing of the LORD to Christians is beneficial (Proverbs 10:22). With the blessings of GOD upon us, we are empowered to prosper in this world, in everything we do (2 Corinthians 8:9; Psalm 1:3; Deuteronomy 28:1-13), given that JESUS has met all the conditions for the blessings to become ours. It is a whole package of blessings.

Because of the blessing:

- We are blessed and we prosper in all that we do. JESUS made HIMSELF poor that we might become rich (2 Corinthians 8:9; Psalm 1:3).

- We are healed and walk in health (Matthew 8:16-17; 1 Peter 2:24; 3 John 1:2: Psalm 103:1).

- We are delivered from the curse of the law (Galatians 3:13) and protected from every harm (Psalm 103:1-4).

- We defeat every enemy that rises against us (Ephesians 6:16); actively fight against the devil, and he will flee from you (James 4:7).

- We are accepted in the beloved and highly favored (*Strong's Concordance*) by GOD (Ephesians 1:6).

- We are righteous and truly holy. (Ephesians 4:24)

- We are chosen and set apart in CHRIST by GOD, to be special to HIM. (Ephesians 1:4).

Psalm 103:1-5 (MSG) gives us more insight into this:

"O my soul, bless God. From head to toe, I'll bless his holy name! O my soul, bless God, don't forget a single blessing! He forgives your sins— everyone. He heals your diseases— everyone. He redeems you from hell— saves your life! He crowns you with love and mercy — a paradise crown. He wraps you in goodness— beauty eternal. He renews your youth— you're always young in his presence."

The Psalm above lists some of the many blessing for believers. JESUS, through paying for and forgiving our sins, and being resurrected from the dead, purely by HIS amazing grace, brought forth all of these wonderful blessings.

Many of our blessings as believers manifest on their own, with little or no contribution from us, and many of such blessings occur for unbelievers too. For example, HIS sun shines on both the believers and unbelievers (Matthew 5:45). However, the blessings that give believers advantage over unbelievers are mostly spiritual and reside in the realm of the spirit (Ephesians 1:3; 1 Corinthians 2:14-15).

JESUS told HIS disciples that some things have been exclusively given to them to know and understand. An example of such are the parables HE used to teach (Mark 4:11; Luke 8:10). Paul talked about the great and marvelous things GOD has prepared for and revealed to His children (1 Corinthians 2:10). The revealed goodies that GOD has for HIS children are mostly in the spiritual realm, and therefore need to be manifested as desired and where they are required. To activate and manifest the spiritual blessings in the physical realm, GOD's children need to learn to exercise their authority.

> The revealed goodies that GOD has for HIS children are mostly in the spiritual realm, and therefore need to be manifested as desired and where they are required.

Everything we receive from GOD is by grace through faith (Romans 4:16; Ephesians 2:8-9), and faith is the "substance of things hoped for, the evidence of things not seen" [Mine: not perceivable with the five senses).

Hebrews 11:1 (KJV)

"Now faith is the substance of things hoped for, the evidence of things not seen."

Hebrews 11:1 (NLT)

"Faith is the confidence that what we hope for will actually happen; it gives us assurance about things we cannot see."

The things hoped for that are not sensate; meaning discernible with the five sense, until they appear in the physical realm, include the blessings, gifts and other things that pertain to life and godliness. Most of these things reside in the spirit realm until you exercise your faith and authority to bring them into the physical world.

To know that with our authority we can cause all our blessings to manifest in the natural world is very important for every Christian.

The Bible is replete with the truth about two realms of realities: the spiritual and the physical world (John 8:23; Ephesians 2:6). Moreover, Verse 3 of Hebrews 11 states that the physical world comes from the invisible (indiscernible with the five senses). Spiritual authority ensures that believers appropriate all that is essential for them to be successful in the earth. To know that with our authority we can cause all our blessings to manifest in the natural world is very important for every Christian. Let's see some of the blessings as revealed from the scriptures:

Believers' Blessings

Genesis 1:26-28 (NKJV)

*26 "Then God said, 'Let us make man in our image, according to our likeness; **let them have dominion** over the fish of the sea, over the birds of the air, and over the cattle, over all the earth and over every creeping thing that creeps on the earth.'*

27 So God created man in HIS [own] image; in the image of God He created him; male and female HE created them.

*28 Then God blessed them, and God said to them, 'Be fruitful and multiply; fill the earth and subdue it; **have dominion** over the fish of the sea, over the birds of the air, and **over every living thing** that moves on the earth.'"*

According to Genesis 1:26-28, man was in charge over all of GOD's creation. Man had power to reproduce/procreate, multiply and have authority over all other inhabitants of the earth.

Deuteronomy 28:1-13 (NKJV) has listed addi-tional blessings of GOD.

1 "Now it shall come to pass, if you diligently obey the voice of the LORD your God, to ob-serve carefully all His commandments which I command you today, that the LORD your God will set you high above all nations of the earth.

2 And all these blessings shall come upon you and overtake you, because you obey the voice of the LORD your God:

3 Blessed [shall] you [be] in the city, and bless-ed [shall] you [be] in the country.

4 Blessed [shall be] the fruit of your body, the produce of your ground and the increase of your herds, the increase of your cattle and the offspring of your flocks.

5 Blessed [shall be] your basket and your kneading bowl.

6 Blessed [shall] you [be] when you come in, and blessed [shall] you [be] when you go out.

7 The LORD will cause your enemies who rise against you to be defeated before your face; they shall come out against you one way and flee before you seven ways.

8 The LORD will command the blessing on you in your storehouses and in all to which you set your hand, and He will bless you in the land which the LORD your God is giving you.

A Divine Privilege

9 The LORD will establish you as a holy people to himself, just as he has sworn to you, if you keep the commandments of the LORD your God and walk in his ways.

*10 Then all peoples of the earth shall see that you are called by the name of the LORD, and **they shall be afraid of you**.*

11 And the LORD will grant you plenty of goods, in the fruit of your body, in the increase of your livestock, and in the produce of your ground, in the land of which the LORD swore to your fathers to give you.

*12 The LORD will open to you His good treasure, the heavens, to give the rain to your land in its season, and **to bless all the work of your hand. You shall lend to many nations, but you shall not borrow**.*

13 And the LORD will make you the head and not the tail; you shall be above only, and not be beneath, if you heed the commandments of the LORD your God, which I command you today, and are careful to observe [them.]"

There are many blessings and privileges given to believers but there are associated conditions that have to be met for the blessings to become realities.

There are many blessings and privileges given to believers in the passage above but there are associated conditions that have to be met for the blessings to become realities. These conditions deter or weaken the confidence of many believers and they doubt the possibilities of these blessings working for them, because they don't think they could ever meet the conditions. Thus, their faith is weakened.

The good news: JESUS CHRIST has fully fulfilled all the conditions for the blessings listed in Deuteronomy 28:1-13 and all other passages in the Bible, and has given GOD's children absolute access to all the blessings of GOD (Galatians 3:29; Romans 8:17). HE also freed us from the curses listed in the rest of Deuteronomy 28 (14-68) by becoming a curse for us (Galatians 3:13). Therefore, as heirs of GOD and joint heirs with CHRIST, we have unlimited and unconditional access to the blessings of GOD. Hallelujah!

> *Revelation 1:5-6 (KJV)*
>
> *"And from Jesus Christ, [who is] the faithful witness, [and] the first begotten of the dead, and the prince of the kings of the earth. Unto him that loved us, and washed us from our sins in his own blood. And hath made us kings and priests unto God and his Father; to him [be] glory and dominion for ever and ever. Amen."*

CHRIST, who was sinless, took the fall for us and

paid our penalty for sin with HIS own blood, made us kings and priests as well as prophets. As kings, we make decrees and they are honored (Mark 11:22-24). As priests, we have direct access to GOD ALMIGHTY any day and any time. HE dwells in us and desires that we enter into HIS rest and dwell peacefully in HIM (Hebrews 4:11; Psalm 91; 15). We have permanent access to HIS presence since we live there because of CHRIST (Hebrews 4:16). As New Testament saints, we are the "prophets of our own lives" (Kenneth Copeland). When we speak the word of faith over our circumstances and situations, we activate the power of GOD to change them to what HE intended them to be (2 Corinthians 4:13; Mark 11:22-24; Isaiah 44:26).

As kings, we make decrees as priests, we have direct access to GOD ALMIGHTY

CHRIST exchanged our sin for HIS righteousness by creating our spirits anew, making us righteous and truly holy (2 Corinthians 5:21; Ephesians 4:24). Consequently, as Christians, we are righteous and holy, not because of our performance, but by His grace (Ephesians 2:8-9). The provision for the blessings in the New Testament is in the past tense because it is already done. GOD has already blessed, not that He will bless – there's a huge difference!

Ephesians 1:3 (KJV)

"Blessed [be] the God and Father of our Lord Jesus Christ, who HATH BLESSED us with all spiritual blessings (with every kind of blessing)

in heavenly [places] in Christ."

Ephesians 1:3 (TPT)

"Every spiritual blessing in the heavenly realm HAS ALREADY BEEN LAVISHED upon us as a love gift from our wonderful heavenly Father, the Father of our Lord Jesus—all because he sees us wrapped into Christ. This is why we celebrate him with all our hearts."

Praise GOD! *The Passion Translation* says that every spiritual blessing in the heavenly realm has already been lavished upon us as a love gift, all because HE sees us, the believers, wrapped into CHRIST.

Whose responsibility it is to enforce obedience to the word of GOD in your circumstances and situations? Of course! You! The question is, why are these blessings not manifesting as GOD has said? Also, did GOD say whose responsibility it is to enforce obedience to the word of GOD in your circumstances and situations? Of course! You! It is your GOD-given responsibility to enforce obedience to the word of GOD in your circumstances, situations and over all satanic forces; but you will not exercise your authority if you don't know that you have the authority to do so. **These blessings and executive privileges** would remain dormant in your spirit man if you didn't acknowledge them and use them (Philemon 1:6).

Ephesians 1: 15-22 contains one of Paul's prayers for the saints in Ephesus. After telling them that they had been blessed with all the spiritual blessings in heavenly places, he prayed that their spiritual eyes and understanding be opened so that they could know what they had in CHRIST JESUS.

Ephesians 1:15-23 (NKJV)

15 "Therefore I also, after I heard of your faith in the Lord Jesus and your love for all the saints,

16 do not cease to give thanks for you, making mention of you in my prayers:

17 that the God of our Lord Jesus Christ, the Father of glory, may give to you the spirit of wisdom and revelation in the knowledge of Him,

18 the eyes of your understanding being enlightened; that you may know what is the hope of His calling, what are the riches of the glory of His inheritance in the saints,

*19 and what [is] the exceeding greatness of His power toward us who believe, according [mine-in proportion to, **in quantity and quality to**] to **the working of His mighty power***

20 which He worked in Christ when He raised Him from the dead and seated [Him] at His right hand in the heavenly [places,]

*21 far above all principality and power and might and dominion, and every name that is named, not only **in this age** but also in that which is to come."*

Paul did not ask GOD to bless the Ephesian Christians, rather that their spiritual eyes be opened to the knowledge of GOD, the hope of the calling of GOD, the riches of what they had inherited in CHRIST, and how great the power of GOD is, the great One, who resides in their spirit man. Paul, by the Spirit, knew that believers could only enjoy the blessings and power of GOD if they knew the authority and power they possess. As soon as Christians become fully aware of, and embrace what is already theirs in CHRIST, knowing the extent of GOD's power in them, they would take advantage of their spiritual authority and live in their blessings.

Therefore, be convinced of the fact that GOD has already given to you all the blessings you will ever require in this life and that the full power of GOD (the power that raised JESUS from the dead) is behind your authority. This should increase your confidence in your authority, and to enjoy all that GOD has given.

Spiritual Authority – the Chief of GOD's Blessings

Do you know you have that authority? Have you been exercising it? Have you been seeing results?

If at this point in your Christian life you don't have testimonies regarding the exercise of your spiritual authority, I trust that if you apply the truths that I am sharing in this book, before long, you will start exercising your authority in CHRIST and seeing results.

Of all the blessings of GOD, in the Old and the New Testaments, spiritual authority tops the list.

Many Christians know vaguely about spiritual authority; some even believe that they have it, but not many make a habit of exercising it.

Of all the blessings of GOD, in the Old and the New Testaments, spiritual authority tops the list. As we discussed in the Introduction, apart from being born again, the spiritual authority given to believers is the most important of the spiritual blessings in heaven and on earth. It is the key to unlocking all the other blessings that we have in CHRIST.

For the Christian, exercising spiritual authority is necessary because GOD's blessings are predicated on this principle.

For the Christian, exercising spiritual authority is necessary because GOD's blessings are predicated on this principle. With the proper use of spiritual authority, a Christian can enforce obedience on demonic agents who

The great news is that as a believer, you have the right to enforce obedience to the word of GOD in any aspect of your life

try to thwart the blessings of GOD from being manifested in his life. We shall see, in Chapter 5, why some blessings could be delayed in manifestation, but the great news is that as a believer, you have the right to enforce obedience to the word of GOD in any aspect of your life where you desire the blessings of GOD.

Ephesians 1:3 tells us that we have already been *"blessed with ALL spiritual blessings in heavenly places,"* but we will not see the result of our blessings including our spiritual authority until we embrace them and form the habit of exercising the authority in our circumstances, situations, and against the activities of satanic spirits.

In summary, you have been blessed and your spiritual authority is the key to unlocking your spiritual blessings. There is no doubt that some of your blessings will naturally manifest by virtue of your new birth. Galatians 3:29 lets us know that when you get born again, you become the seed of Abraham. This means that all the blessings of Abraham are yours, and GOD, guaranteeing that you will get the blessings HE promised Abraham, sealed it with an oath, "saying, 'Surely blessing I will bless you, and multiplying I will multiply you." (Hebrews 6:14 NKJV). (See Genesis 22 for details). That promise to Abraham, GOD has fulfilled through

CHRIST, to believers who would come to HIM in faith.

Hebrews 6:17 affirms that GOD specifically swore to fulfill the promise HE made to Abraham unto the "heirs of promise", because HE was "willing more abundantly" to convince them about the immutability of HIS promise. The heirs of the promise, according to Galatians 3:29 are Christians, because they belong to CHRIST. And if you are CHRIST's, then you are Abraham's seed and heirs according to the promise.

> *Hebrews 6:13 -18*
>
> *13 "For when God made a promise to Abraham, because He could swear by no greater, He swore by Himself,*
>
> *14 saying, 'Surely blessing, I will bless you and multiplying I will multiply you.'*
>
> *15 And so after he had patiently endured, he obtained the promise.*
>
> *16 For men indeed swear by the greater, and an oath for confirmation is for them an end of all dispute.*
>
> *17 Thus God determining to show more abundantly to the heirs of promise the immutability of His counsel, confirmed it by an oath,*
>
> *18 that by two immutable things, in which it is impossible for God to lie, we might have strong consolation, who have fled for refuge to lay hold of the hope set before us."*

The most fascinating fact is that GOD is very enthusiastic to show us that we are heirs of HIS kingdom and notify us of our blessings. **For this reason, GOD swore or made an oath**, so that we, of the new covenant, would never doubt that the blessings are ours as well. GOD is amazing; this implies that we are blessed always, because CHRIST has fulfilled and paid all the debts that we couldn't pay.

My brothers and sisters, GOD's promises to you are immutable; that means that they are unchangeable. They don't depend on your performance, only on your acceptance or belief. If you believe that you have them, they are yours to use and manifest HIS blessings in your life and the lives of others in your circle of influence. GOD made the oath, not just for Abraham's sake, but for you, the heirs of promise. The singular reason GOD ALMIGHTY, the GREAT I AM, the CREATOR of heaven and earth, swore concerning HIS blessings, was so that you and I would never doubt that these blessings are for us too! Praise the LORD!

Knowing that you have authority is the first step; then, embracing and exercising it launch you into victorious Christian living.

Therefore, you are blessed and that blessing is as sure as day and night. The top of the blessings is your spiritual authority, with which you can enforce compliance for every blessing that is in the Word of GOD. For example, According to Luke 10:19, and Mark 16:17 you have authority over all devils and to cast them out. Make a conscious effort to exercise your authority and begin to see the power of GOD manifest in your life. Knowing that you have authority is the first step; then, embracing and exercising it launch you into victorious Christian living.

CHAPTER 3

BASIS FOR EXERCISING SPIRITUAL AUTHORITY

The Christian's understanding and establishment in exercising of spiritual authority are rooted in three crucial foundational principles:

1. Functional knowledge of the act of being born again.

2. A functional understanding of the three-part being of man (spirit, soul, and body).

3. Absolute dependence on the word of GOD.

The Act of Being Born Again

John 3:1-6 (NKJV)

1 "There was a man of the Pharisees named Nicodemus, a ruler of the Jews.

2 This man came to Jesus by night and said to Him, 'Rabbi, we know that You are a teacher come from God; for no one can do these signs that You do unless God is with him.'

3 Jesus answered and said to him, 'Most assuredly, I say to you, unless one is born again, he cannot see the kingdom of God.'

4 Nicodemus said to Him, 'How can a man be born when he is old? Can he enter a second time into his mother's womb and be born?'

5 Jesus answered, 'Most assuredly, I say to you, unless one is born of water and the Spirit, he cannot enter the kingdom of God.

6 'That which is born of the flesh is flesh, and that which is born of the Spirit is spirit.'"

Some Christians' response to spirits and the spiritual realm makes it obvious that they do not understand what it means to be born again. For many, "born again" is a phrase usually thrown around by religious fanatics, who are unintelligible, lazy, irrational, and gullible. Some others, who recognize that JESUS HIMSELF presented being born again as a prerequisite to gain access to the kingdom of Heaven, reduce the born-again experience to a mere humanistic event of being baptized in water; a mere symbolism that represents the burial and resurrection of JESUS CHRIST. This is evidence that they don't understand the phenomenon called being "born again". Many unbelievers claim to know what it means to be born again, and in their erroneous understanding, they pass judgement on born-again Christians.

To be effective in our position as sons of GOD, we need to understand what it means to be born again. Before I discuss what being born again means, let's look at what it is not.

1. *Being born again does just not mean receiving JESUS as your personal LORD and SAVIOR. Receiving JESUS as your personal LORD and SAVIOR is a stage in the process of how you become born again.*

2. *Being born again does not mean living a righteous lifestyle, although you are empowered to live righteously when you are born again.*

3. *Being born again is not being baptized by water, although you are expected to be water baptized if you are born again. Because of Mark 16:16, many teach that you must be water baptized to be born again but that is not what it means. Even if Mark 16:16 could be taken literally, it would only show the physical significance of being born again, not the meaning behind it.*

Literally, being born again implies at least one previous birth. In John 3:6, JESUS suggests two births: being born of the flesh and being born of the Spirit. The first time a man is born, it is by his parents (John 1:12-13). A man and his wife make the decision to conceive and give birth to a child. In this case, flesh gives birth to flesh, because the earthly child is housed in a fleshly body. In this first biological birth, you didn't have a choice of when, where, how, or to whom you were born.

However, in the new birth, which we call being "born again", the Spirit of GOD gives birth to a brand new spirit in you. This spirit is the REAL you. The real you is not the person you see in the mirror. It is the spiritual part of you that escapes out of your body when you die (James 2:26). John 4:24 says that GOD is a spirit, so HE gives birth to spirits, and you become one of them at your new birth.

John 4:24 says that GOD is a spirit, so HE gives birth to spirits, and you become one of them at your new birth.

When a child is born to his parents, regardless of how righteous, holy or innocent the person appears at birth, the spirit within that new baby is dead (Genesis 2:17, 3:6-7). This means that the baby is spiritually separated from GOD (Ephesians 2; 12; Romans 5:12) because of sin (Romans 3:23, 6:23, 7:9, 11; Ephesians 2:1 & 5). Does it mean that babies and little children end up in hell? No! It means that as soon as they are of age, they too need to be born again

The New Testament does not have prescribed age children are required to get born again. We saw JESUS insisting that little children must not be prevented from hearing HIM or the gospel (Matthew 19:14; Mark 10:14; Luke 18:16). Adam's sin passed upon all men, meaning everyone on earth became a sinner by inheriting Adam and Eve's sin from the garden of Eden (Romans 5:12). Does it mean that children go to hell when they die young? No! Praise GOD!

JESUS said In Matthew 18:3: "Truly, I say to you, unless you turn and become like children, you will never enter the kingdom of heaven" and in Matthew 19:14, "the Kingdom of Heaven belongs to those who are like these children." Therefore, babies and little children would enter heaven. Besides, since JESUS fully paid for the sins of everyone, including the babies, and we are saved "not by the work of righteousness which we have done" (Titus 3:4), the children below the age of accountability receive justification by grace (Titus 3:4-7)

The person's spirit was "dead in trespasses and sins" (Ephesians 2:1), and it was subject to the god of this world, satan (Ephesians 2:2-3). Moreover, according to Genesis 8:21," the imagination of man's heart's heart is evil from their youth." Thus, everyone born into this world has a proclivity for evil from birth.

Genesis 8:21 (NLT)

And the LORD was pleased with the aroma of

the sacrifice and said to himself, "I will never again curse the ground because of the human race, even though everything they think or imagine is bent toward evil from childhood. I will never again destroy all living things."

The ranking in the spiritual realm resembles the ranking in the physical. President Mohamadu Buhari of Nigeria is the highest-ranking person in Nigeria today, and President Donald J. Trump is the highest ranking person in the U.S.A. Everyone else ranks below their respective presidents. GOD is the highest in the spiritual realm (Genesis 1:1). GOD is the most high; HE is not just above all gods, but the most high, Period! The angels follow (Hebrews 1:4; 13-14; etc.), before satan and his demons (Ephesians 2:2-3; Romans 6:16; etc.) Below satan is the spirit of the unregenerate man (Ephesians 2:2-3; Romans 6:16; 2 Corinthians 4:4). That is why the unregenerate man is subject to satan until he gets born again (Colossians 1:3). Then, he is translated from satan's kingdom (from under satan) into CHRIST, at the right hand of the FATHER, in heavenly places (Ephesians 2:6). You become born again by believing in our LORD JESUS CHRIST and confessing that HE is alive in you (Romans 10:9-10). This is what many call receiving JESUS CHRIST as your personal LORD and SAVIOR (John 1:12).

At the second birth, new birth, spiritual birth, or being

born of GOD—when one gets born again—GOD quickens, (Ephesians 2:5) gives birth to (John 3:6) and creates a brand new spirit (Ephesians 4:24) in a person and that person spiritually becomes a brand new person, i.e. old things pass away, and all things become brand new (2 Corinthians 5:17). It is a supernatural phenomenon; It is all done by GOD! Praise JESUS!

John 1:12-13 explicitly explains that this second birth is NOT by the will of man but is conceived and executed by GOD! Thus, to be born again means to be birthed by the Spirit of GOD (John 3:6). GOD is a Spirit (John 4:24), therefore whoever is born of GOD is a spirit, a "living soul" – meaning a man with a living spirit (Genesis 2:7; 1Corinthians 15:45); a man that houses the Spirit of GOD (1 Corinthians 6:19; Galatians 4:6; Ephesians 1:13).

Once you become born again, you are a spirit (John 3:6) that gets translated from under satan to a level not just above satan and the angels but to the same level as the Son of GOD (in CHRIST) at the right hand of GOD (Ephesians 2:6). Praise the LORD!

Being born again is a spiritual birth. It is GOD, giving birth to a brand-new spirit in man, so the man becomes a son of GOD (John 1:12). The brand new born-again spirit of man is created righteous and "truly holy" (Ephesians 4:24). Subsequently, the new man receives the Spirit of CHRIST in his brand new spirit (Galatians 4:6). Then, that brand new, born-again spirit is "sealed with the HOLY SPIRIT of promise" according to Ephesians 1:13. That brand new you, the spirit that has been fused with the Spirit of CHRIST and sealed with the HOLY SPIRIT, cannot commit sin (1 John 3:9).

According to 1 Corinthians 6:17, the person who is united to the LORD becomes one Spirit with **As CHRIST is, so are you in this world!** HIM. In other words, a born-again spirit in a Christian is one Spirit with CHRIST. Spiritually speaking, you are one with JESUS CHRIST. Praise GOD!

What this means is that you, as a born again Christian, share the same Spirit with JESUS CHRIST! No wonder 1 John 4:17b says that as CHRIST is, so are you in this world! 1 Corinthians 6:17 makes a profound statement that ought to make every born-again Christian scream for joy. The scripture here admonishes born-again Christians not to join themselves with people who are not their spouses in adultery or fornication, because they are spiritually joined with the LORD! This literally means that your born-again spirit is intimately united with the Spirit of CHRIST. No wonder the LORD says, "I will never leave you nor forsake you," (Hebrews 13:5) because HE does not just visit but abides (resides or lives inside of you) to the point of being one spirit with you! This is union! This is love!

Literally, when you got born again, although you may

not have felt anything physically, something supernatural happened! GOD, who became man for the sole purpose of securing your salvation, becomes one spirit with you! The union of the spirit of CHRIST and the born-again spirit has tremendous spiritual and physical implications, the first of which is the restoration of the authority back to man, at least on the level it was in the Garden of Eden. Being born again is a mysterious birth, and it gives us special privileges. *"But as many as received HIM, to them gave HE power to become the sons of GOD"* (John 1:12). It is a gift. GOD gives us the privilege –the legal right – to become sons of GOD, with the authority and power of GOD!

Being born again makes carnal men sons of GOD, with the same authority and power of JESUS CHRIST. As a son of GOD, you are a joint heir with CHRIST (Galatians 4:7; Romans 8:17). The exact same power that raised JESUS from the dead dwells in the born-again spirit of man (Ephesians 1:19), and you have legal access to all that JESUS owns. Praise the LORD!

A Functional Understanding of the Three-part Being of Man (Spirit, Soul and Body)

Without a functional understanding of the concept of

spirit, soul, and body as it relates to Christianity, and the proper understanding of who a born-again Christian really is and what he has, it is almost impossible for a Christian to manifest the power and glory of GOD fully, constantly, and regularly.

The truth is that man is a spirit, has a soul, and lives in a body. This provides a solid foundation for understanding the Bible and provides insight into the part of man that GOD addresses in the Bible.

1 Thessalonians 5:23 (KJV) is one of the Bible passages, that spells it out: it says, *"And the very God of peace sanctify you wholly; and [I pray God] your whole spirit and soul and body be preserved blameless unto the coming of our Lord Jesus Christ."*

There is no doubt that a man is the sum total of a spirit, a soul and a body. However, that is not what is believed, generally in Christendom. This revelation is not very common to many men and women of GOD. Thanks to one of our present-day GOD's Generals, Andrew Wommack, who heralded this concept and has made it popular today. (To read more about the concept of the spirit, soul and body of a Christian, read Andrew's *Spirit, Soul, and Body)*.

The Greek word "Pneuma" means more than the "rational soul" representing a human (*Strong's Concordance*). It means the spirit or inner man, the part of man that is in direct communication with the Spirit of GOD (Wommack, 2005). The real you is your spirit. That is the only part of you that got born again instantly when you said yes to CHRIST. Your spirit was what became brand new, in accordance with 2 Corinthians 5:17, not your soul and not your body. It is the part of you that when it leaves your body, you cease to breath and cease to live in this world.

Man has three parts: spirit, soul, and body. The body is very obvious. What you see when you look into a mirror is your body. If you are looking at me face to face and talking to me, you will be looking at my body but you will be speaking to my soul, which is my mind, mental, and emotional part. Your soul is a sum total of your mind, will, emotions, conscience and mental part of you – it is all that is described as your personality (Wommack, 2005).

You can access your body and your soul with your physical senses (taste, hear, smell, feel, and see) at any given time, but not your spirit. You can feel and touch your physical body but you can also be touched by words that someone speaks to you, depending on what they said.

A good example is this book. Even though you are not seeing me right now with your physical eyes, I am touching you with the word of GOD that you are reading. I was able to touch many through my radio broadcasts when they listened. Many called and said that the words they heard touched them so much that they bowed their knees and praised the LORD, or gave their hearts to CHRIST in their bedrooms, living rooms or in their cars. The part of you that was touched with the words I preached was your soul. Your ears bring the words into your mind and process the words; your mental parts get an understanding, your emotion carries the expression of what you believe you heard; your will determines your response, and when you try to resist, the power of the HOLY SPIRIT prompts you to respond by giving your heart to the LORD. And when you tried to resist it, your conscience kept the urge burning in your mind. I did not physically touch you but I touched you with the words you read or heard through the radio broadcast or this book. I can also touch your emotions. I can either make you glad or I can make you sad depending on your perspective on what I said.

My point is that you can say something and hurt a person or make them excited. I am sure you've all experienced it sometimes when you were offended by what someone said. Or you must have heard someone say that what you said to them hurt them. You didn't physically touch them but you did touch them with the words that you spoke. You can make someone glad or sad with words. All of that happens in the soul of man.

Just like your body, most human beings are in touch with their souls. You can consciously process information to get an understanding and then respond accordingly, based on your decision, from your will. All of that takes place in your soul. You can tell if you are sad, angry or neither. You can physically access your soul and your body.

So, the soul and the body can be accessed by every normal being, at any given time, but you cannot access your born-again spirit the same way. The Spirit of a Christian cannot be accessed like the soul and body of man. JESUS said something about the process of explaining the new birth; JESUS said, "That which is born of the Spirit is spirit, and that which is born of flesh is flesh."

What JESUS was saying is that spirit is spirit and flesh is flesh (John 3:6) and there is no direct connection between the two. They are connected in some ways that we will be expatiating on later, but the point is that there is no direct, natural way the flesh can access the spirit. In other words, the spirit is not easily accessible directly by any natural or physical means. As I mentioned above, if you want to know how your body feels, all you need to do is think and you can articulate how you feel in your body: whether you are tired or full of energy, cold, or hot, feeling pain, itching, or whether you are excited or happy. You have a constant and instant access to your body without any special request. Your mind constantly feeds you with the information about how you feel in your body.

The same is true of your soul. You don't need a prophet to tell if you are afraid, happy, depressed, fussy, confused, frustrated, or mentally alert within your own mind. When you see a mathematical problem, no one can tell you if you can solve it or not; your mind will let you know. But your spirit is not the same as your body or soul. Your spirit cannot be contacted through any of your physical senses. You cannot feel, see, hear, smell, or taste your spirit. It is not sensate. The spirit cannot be directly accessed by any physical, natural way. This is one of the greatest realities of Christianity: the spirit of man is what got born again at the new birth. It was not the body and it was not the soul.

Before I understood this concept of spirit, soul and body, I used to participate in what my church called "soul winning." In our churches, we had "soul winners." What they meant, was winning a person to CHRIST, but the choice of words has made many Christians, like myself, think that the soul of man is what gets born again. No! It is the spirit of man. This misunderstanding creates confusion, wrong teaching and wrong belief systems in Christendom. It is the spirit of a man through which GOD communicates with man (Proverbs 20:27; Roman's 8:16), and this is what gets born again at the new birth. The spirit is the part of us that the power and the life of GOD flows through.

If a Christian does not understand that they can't feel or access spiritual realities through their physical senses, they become confused. If a Christian does not understand the concept of spirit, soul, and body, they may go to the mirror to see if they are a brand-new creature, or try to access their physical body, looking for the power of GOD. When this fails, some may get disappointed, and begin to think, "Maybe the Bible doesn't really mean what it says."

I believe that many denominations and ministers of GOD who don't believe that genuine miracles of GOD are still here today, got to that point because they don't under-

It is a dangerous thing to try to evaluate spiritual realities through physical, natural means.

stand that "spirit is spirit, and flesh is flesh," and there is no direct connection between the two. It is a dangerous thing to try to evaluate spiritual realities through physical, natural means. Spiritual things must be spiritually discerned (1 Corinthians 2:14).

My dear brothers and sisters, GOD is not a man that HE should lie (Numbers 23:19; Hebrew 6:18). Men lie, but GOD doesn't! If HE says that the power of GOD lives inside of you, guess what? The power of GOD lives inside of you. Praise the LORD!

The power of GOD lives inside of you

Many people try to compare their personal experiences with what GOD says in the Bible and when they don't match up, they get disappointed and discouraged. Some would then either complain that the Bible is difficult to understand or that the Bible is not true. Some pray and ask GOD for HIS power, for example, and when they don't feel powerful, or hear an audible voice of GOD saying, "My son or daughter, behold, I have given you power," they immediately conclude that they don't have the power. Many of the variations of Christianity and many of the gimmicks in the church today, stem from this confusion.

However, the truth is that GOD has already given you a born again spirit, with the exact same power that raised JESUS from the dead (Ephesians 1:19). So, asking GOD to give you what HE has already given, stems from unbelief or ignorance. You should pray, like Paul prayed for the Ephesian church, to open the eyes of your understanding.

To access the spirit, you have to believe only! (Mark 5:36; Philemon 1:6). Believing in what you cannot access with your physical senses is a spiritual exercise. Faith is an element of the fruit of the spirit, therefore it is of the spirit (Galatians 5:22). That is why you can't feel faith. Faith is translated into your mind by the word "believe".

JESUS was explicit when HE said, "ONLY BELIEVE!" Belief is what I call the sixth sense that a born-again Christian should live by. And

> **Belief is what I call the sixth sense that a born-again Christian should live by.**

this is expressed throughout the Bible by the word "faith." "The just shall live by faith," (Habakkuk 2:4; Romans 1:17; Galatians 3:11; Hebrews 10:38) is a biblical truth, declared explicitly four times in the Bible and succinctly conveys the "how" to live victoriously as a Christian. "Have faith in GOD"! The just shall live by faith (by his faith in GOD), Mark 11:22. (See also: Mark 9:23; 2 Chronicles 20:20; Psalm 62:8; John 14:1). Without faith it is impossible to please GOD (Hebrews 11:6b).

JUST A NOTE OF CAUTION! CHRISTIANS ARE NOT THE ONLY PEOPLE THAT HAVE ACCESS TO THE SPIRIT REALM, BUT THEY ARE THE ONLY ONES THAT HAVE ACCESS TO THE SPIRIT OF GOD, THROUGH OUR LORD JESUS CHRIST.

John 14:6 (KJV)

"Jesus said unto him, I am the way, the truth, and the life: no man cometh unto the Father, but by me."

PRAISE THE LORD! JESUS IS THE KING OF THE SPIRIT WORLD, HE IS IN CHARGE! HE HAS ALL THE POWER! AND WITH HIM, WE HAVE ALL THE POWER!

Psalms 62:11 (KJV)

"God hath spoken once; twice have I heard this; that power belonged unto God."

Thanks be to CHRIST who has given us access to the power of GOD through our born-again spirit. However, test every spirit; every spirit that does not confess that JESUS came in the flesh is not of GOD (1 John 4:2-3).

In conclusion, my brethren, you have authority and the power of GOD to live a victorious Christian life. Step out in faith and trust the LORD to see you through to victory!

Absolute Trust and Dependence on the Word of GOD

The first reason to trust the Word of GOD is because GOD said so! The fact that GOD said anything is a necessary and sufficient reason to believe it and to do it! The kingdom of GOD operates by laws and the laws are the words of GOD. GOD binds HIMSELF by HIS word which HE does not break (Psalm 89:34). Not only does GOD not break

The word of GOD will NEVER return to GOD void, without accomplishing what it is sent to accomplish.

HIS word, HIS word also does not break itself. The word of GOD will NEVER return to GOD void, without accomplishing what it is sent to accomplish (Isaiah 55:11). Because it is impossible for GOD to lie (Hebrews 6:18).

Every word of GOD contains enough active ingredients to accomplish its mission to whoever, wherever and for whomever it was spoken and wherever it was believed. Satan and his agents CANNOT break or cause the word of GOD not to be established (Matthew 4:4, 6, 10; Luke 4: 8,

12). This is the primary reason satan is afraid of any Christian who believes the word of GOD. The Bible testifies that GOD has magnified HIS word above all HIS name (Psalm 138:2). GOD has a name that manifests differently and severally, but HIS Word is magnified "above all HIS name."

GOD ALMIGHTY, JESUS CHRIST, HOLY GHOST, JEHOVAH, etc., are some of the names by which GOD is known. Psalm 138 says that the word of GOD is magnified above all the names by which we can refer to HIM.

Several scriptures tell us about the power that is in the name of JESUS and that is the truth (Philippians 2:9-10). This is not diminishing the power that is in the name of JESUS by any stretch, but rather, establishing equality of the power of the name to the power of HIS word. *"...the Word was made flesh, and dwelt among us, (and we beheld HIS glory, the glory as of the only begotten of the FATHER) full of grace and truth."* (John 1:14). This is JESUS CHRIST! Praise the LORD!

Romans 14:11 (KJV)

"For it is written, [As] I live, saith the Lord, every knee shall bow to me, and every tongue shall confess to God."

So, we know that at the name of JESUS, every knee will bow and every tongue shall confess that JESUS is LORD (Romans 14:11). Additionally, the word of GOD is like a hammer that breaks any rock into pieces and it is like a fire that burns off anything that wants to establish itself above the knowledge of GOD (Jeremiah 23:28-29; 2 Corinthians 10:4-5; Ephesians 6:14-15). This includes dreams, prophecies, visions, negative thoughts and so forth, not supported by the word of GOD.

> *John 1:1-3*
>
> *1 "In the beginning was the Word, and the Word was with God, and the Word was God.*
>
> *2 The same was in the beginning with God.*
>
> *3 All things were made by Him; and without Him was not anything made that was made."*

The Word of GOD is GOD! This should help you understand why the Word always works if you believe it. Doesn't the Bible say that all things are possible to him that believes (Mark 9:23)? From the scriptures above, you can agree that all things are possible to those who believe HIS Word! The Word of GOD is spirit and life (John 6:63). This means that GOD's word can penetrate anywhere unhindered, and it gives life. The Word is "quick and powerful" (Hebrews 4:12), therefore it can not only penetrate all things, but it is powerful enough to quicken and give life to all dead things. Believe it, speak it faithfully, and you shall have whatsoever you say! Praise the Living GOD!

In summary, what GOD says is constant, consistent, stable and universal, for everyone, everywhere, under the same conditions. Therefore, the Word of GOD is LAW. It can be trusted to work every single time the necessary conditions are met.

It can be trusted to work every single time the necessary conditions are met.

Praise the LORD! Just as the physical world operates under laws (physical laws, like gravitational laws, judiciary laws of the land, customary laws, etc.), the kingdom of GOD operates under spiritual laws as well.

GOD is the one who established all spiritual, physical and moral laws that even HE will not break, and the spiritual laws are the word of GOD. GOD established moral laws: the laws that tell us how human beings are supposed to behave, though they often don't behave that way (C.S. Lewis, *Mere Christianity*). Scientists discover physical laws: the laws of how material things work when the established conditions are met, and GOD made all. When GOD says something, it becomes a legal, binding contract.

When GOD says something, it becomes a legal, binding contract.

Psalm 89:34

"My covenant will I not break, nor alter the thing that is gone out of my lips."

My dear brothers and sisters, GOD will not honor the spiritual authority you command, except it is based on the word of GOD. Prayers like "back to sender" and "GOD, bring down fire" on your enemies are not of GOD, and they don't work. To respond with the word of GOD that you believe will work – always. For example, a word-based response to someone who pronounces a curse on you is: *"A curse ceaseless shall not come to me"* (Proverbs 26:2b), or *"No weapon formed against me shall prosper"* (Isaiah 54:17), or *"CHRIST has delivered me from the curse of the law (Galatians 3:13); I am blessed"* (Ephesians 1:3), and I cannot be cursed!

If you stand on the word of GOD and believe it, then no plan and purpose of the enemy against you can EVER prosper. When GOD speaks, it becomes a covenant, meaning it is a contract! HE will not break it. JESUS upholds "**all things** by the word of his power" (Hebrews 1:3). Anything that can hold the universe together is powerful enough to deal with your much smaller world; you can depend on the truth of the WORD!

Think about it! If the power of the word of GOD is what holds the world together (and this is the truth) then, if GOD ever defaults in keeping HIS own word, the world will crash. In other words, our entire universe is being held together by the integrity and power of GOD's Word. If HE were ever to break a promise or otherwise violate HIS Word, the entire universe, and you and I, would be destroyed.

Whatever GOD says becomes a contract – a law. It is GOD'S word that holds everything together. Whatever GOD says becomes a contract – a law. Once HE says it,

HE will not change it. To effectively use your authority, you must know this truth and what HIS laws are; you must read, understand and accept what the Bible says concerning you.

Therefore, if you align yourself with the word of GOD in meeting the necessary conditions that it requires, the Word will produce for you, physically and spiritually, whatever it is sent to accomplish! This is not being legalistic, neither is it the same thing as a performance-based relationship with GOD. You are not meeting the conditions of faith so that GOD can love you or give you anything. No, that's all by grace. What I am talking about here has to do with works that demonstrate your faith.

As Andrew Wommack puts it, you are not saved by works, but faith does not exist without the works that express it. For example, if you never believed in JESUS CHRIST as the Son of GOD; although the grace that brought salvation is available for you, you will not be born again. Believing in JESUS CHRIST is a work that demonstrates your faith, and it produces the resultant consequence of being born of the spirit. The actions that follow your beliefs operationalize your faith. Those actions bring into operations your faith; in other words, the actions put into effect or make your belief work. Otherwise, your faith is comatose or dead (James 2:26).

John 6:28-29 (NKJV)

28 "Then they said to Him, 'What shall we do,

that we may work the works of God?'

29 Jesus answered and said to them, 'This is the work of God, that you believe in Him whom He sent.'"

A young lawyer asked JESUS what he could do that would constitute the works of GOD. JESUS told him to believe in HIM. Based on the man's question, anyone could be fooled into thinking that he had already believed in GOD and just wanted to know what else he could do for GOD. JESUS responded by asking him to demonstrate that he believed in GOD by believing in HE, whom GOD had sent – JESUS!

By the same token, there are conditions for the word of GOD to be productive in your life. You must believe the words that GOD has spoken concerning you! You must acknowledge the things that HE has given you! You must think, speak and act like they are yours, and they will truly become yours in manifestation! That victory glorifies GOD!

You must think, speak and act like they are yours,

We know GOD and JESUS abided by the word of GOD, spoke it, lived by it, enforced it, and manifested it. We can conclude that victory and success in exercising our spiritual authority can be achieved only by abiding in and by the word of GOD (Joshua 1:8).

CHAPTER 4

YOU ARE A SPIRIT

1 Thessalonians 5:23 (KJV)

"And the very God of peace sanctify you wholly; and [I pray God] your whole spirit and soul and body be preserved blameless unto the coming of our Lord Jesus Christ."

At the beginning, (Genesis 2:7; Genesis 5:2) man was created a tripartite being (a spirit, with a soul and living in a body). But when man inadvertently rejected the leadership of GOD, his spirit died and everyone born into the world after Adam and Eve, came only with a "dead" spirit (a human spirit that is separated from the Spirit of GOD), having a soul and living in a body.

If you are born again then you are born of GOD; if you are born of GOD, then you are born of the Spirit of GOD (John 4:24). You are a spirit because that which is born of the Spirit is spirit (John 3:6). The big question is: do you see yourself as a spirit?

I once taught a series on the radio titled, "The Reality About Christianity." What motivated me to develop the series was that I noticed that many Christians do not know who they are and are living below their full potentials in CHRIST.

We are spirits and this fact is not something unnerving. We can spiritually influence things that are outside our immediate location, ranging from the next room, to millions of miles away. We do this with prayers and speaking faith-filled words. As a matter of fact, that is why, as Christians, we need to make prayer an integral part of our lives. We don't see GOD physically, but we know we can always reach HIM when we pray. We also need to realize that we remotely control circumstances, situations and spirits, with our prayers and words of faith.

Let me illustrate. In the early hours of September 6th, 2004, I was praying in my house that was located close to Detroit, Michigan.

After praying in tongues for some time, I overheard myself praying out in my understanding, and I was saying, "Give her oxygen and she will live." I was startled, but I thanked GOD for the newborn baby, for I had inner witness in my spirit that I was praying for a newborn baby. None of my relatives, friends and acquaintances was pregnant or due to give birth, so I just thanked the LORD for whoever the prayer was for.

Not long after, a relative and friend visited me from Washington State, on his way to attend the Christening of a new baby and I went with him. Interestingly, I was told the story of the child whose christening we had come for. Shiloh is the name of the child. She was stillborn at birth in Lansing, on the same day and time that I was praying in my house. Lansing is the capital of Michigan and is located about one hundred miles away from my home. Shiloh's mother testified that Shiloh started breathing after she was given oxygen, which was orchestrated by a voice they all heard in the delivery room: "Give her oxygen and she will live." Praise the LORD!

The truth is that Christians are powerful spirits that have been elevated to the right hand of GOD in the heavenly places in CHRIST. Sadly, some are not always conscious of this and most times are too busy, distracted or ignorant to live in this realm, therefore they are forced to depend solely on their humanity.

John 3:1-6 (NKJV)

1 "There was a man of the Pharisees named Nicodemus, a ruler of the Jews.

2 This man came to Jesus by night and said to Him, 'Rabbi, we know that you are a teacher come from God; for no one can do these signs that you do unless God is with him.'

3 Jesus answered and said to him, 'Most assur-

edly, I say to you, unless one is born again, he cannot see the kingdom of God.'

4 Nicodemus said to Him, 'How can a man be born when he is old? Can he enter a second time into his mother's womb and be born?'

5 Jesus answered, 'Most assuredly, I say to you, unless one is born of water and the Spirit, he cannot enter the kingdom of God.

6 'That which is born of the flesh is flesh, and that which is born of the Spirit is spirit.'"

Christians are given spiritual authority because they are spirits. JESUS emphasized to Nicodemus, a Jewish religious leader, that he must be born again to gain entrance into the Kingdom of GOD. In verse 5 above, He explained that entering into the Kingdom of GOD requires being born of water and of the Spirit, and that which is born of flesh is flesh and what is born of Spirit is spirit. JESUS was basically saying that there are two types of birth: human beings (flesh) birthing their kind, and GOD, who is a SPIRIT (referenced in the passage) giving birth to a spirit – the born again person.

The Importance of Seeing Yourself as a Spirit

Galatians 4:6-7

"And because you are sons, God has sent forth the spirit of his son into your hearts crying out,

Abba Father! Therefore you are no longer a slave but a son and if a son then an heir of God through Christ."

Your spirit houses the Spirit of CHRIST, so you can't commit sin because you are born of GOD (1 John 3:9). According to Ephesians 4:24, your spirit was created righteous and truly holy, at the new birth. Your default state as a spirit is righteous and truly holy; it was created free from sin and incapable of committing sin (ibid).

If you don't understand that you are a spirit, you will read the scriptures without understanding them, but because you are a spirit, you possess a soul and you live in a body. The Bible is written to address the totality of your being, that is, the spirit, soul and body. When you understand this, you will ascertain what aspect of you a particular scripture is addressing at a specified time. For example, Romans 12:2 that says, *"be ye transformed by the renewing of your mind,"* addresses explicitly the soul. It is not talking about your spirit, because your spirit was created perfect at the new birth, and therefore does not need renewal.

The Bible is full of expressions that portray children of GOD as spirits, but not many Christians see themselves as spirits. Christians, who don't see themselves as spirits, are not spiritually minded.

As a spirit, you are able to appreciate your spirituality more than your humanity,

Because of this, they wrongly evaluate the spiritual implications of things; they see things only physically. As a spirit, you are able to appreciate your spirituality more than your humanity, and this causes you to be more conscious of who you are in CHRIST, and hence exhibit more power. As you walk in faith like this, GOD is pleased.

Romans 8:8 says that those who are carnally minded cannot please GOD. To be carnal does not necessarily mean sinful, but it includes being materialistic or humanistic in your approach to things. On the other hand, seeing yourself as a spirit being would make you inclined to using your spiritual authority more than relying on your humanity. This keeps you in charge, in the realm of the spirit, and you are in a better position to make changes better, and probably faster.

Seeing yourself as a spirit also helps you understand that your influence changes the circumstances, situations and activities of other spirits. Distance, barriers and heights cannot stop you from reaching your target of interest.

Mindset Change

Romans 12:1-2 (NKJV)

1 "I beseech you therefore, brethren, by the mercies of God, that you present your bodies a living sacrifice, holy, acceptable to God, [which is] your reasonable service.

*2 And do not be conformed to this world, but be transformed by the **renewing of your mind**, that you may prove what [is] that good and acceptable and perfect will of God."*

The phrase "renewing your mind", in the passage above, is addressed to a part of the human soul – the mind. This scripture is not addressing your spirit, simply because you can't renew something that is already perfect. Your born again spirit was created anew, "righteous and truly holy" (Ephesians 4:24). It came perfect in every way, created after the image of GOD.

On the other hand, the soul has to be renewed because its state before the new birth was corrupt, depraved and carnal, materialistic, bound to the human body, and incapable of aligning perfectly with the Spirit of GOD in you. (Romans 12:2-3). Your soul is made up of your mind, will, intellect, emotion, conscience and feelings. The Bible instructs Christians to renew their minds with the word of GOD, and the renewed mind can apprise the will, the emotion and the conscience. The mind is extremely important in accessing all the blessings and in realizing all the transformations in the life of a Christian.

Adequately Evaluate All Situations

Salvation guarantees heaven for the believer but does not guarantee inoculation against the devil's attacks. GOD is a spirit; so also is satan, and his attacks on believers are best addressed in the spiritual realm. As a spirit being, the Christian should properly evaluate circumstances and situations, to determine the best spiritual strategy or course of action to use in the event of any attack from the enemy.

Ephesians 2:1-6 (NKJV)

1 "And you [He made alive,] who were dead in trespasses and sins,

2 in which you once walked according to the course of this world, according to the prince of the power of the air, the spirit who now works in the sons of disobedience,

3 among whom also we all once conducted ourselves in the lusts of our flesh, fulfilling the desires of the flesh and of the mind, and were by nature children of wrath, just as the others.

4 But God, who is rich in mercy, because of His great love with which He loved us, 5 even when we were dead in trespasses, made us alive together with Christ (by grace you have

You are a Spirit

been saved),

6 and raised [us] up together, and made [us] sit together in the heavenly [places] in Christ Jesus."

In Ephesians 2, the Bible discloses how satan, "the spirit at work in the hearts of those who refuse to obey GOD" (NLT), is responsible for the blinders in the eyes of unbelievers and those who live in defiance to the Spirit of GOD. Verse 6 shows that the born-again spirit of man has been quickened, raised up altogether with CHRIST and is seated together at the right hand of GOD in heavenly places.

Before your conversion, the spirit within you was dead (separated from the HOLY SPIRIT) (Genesis 2:16-17; Ephesians 2:1-3), then a brand-new spirit was created within you, by the Spirit of GOD, and you were resurrected with CHRIST and made to sit in the heavenly places. Before it was created anew, righteous and truly holy, it was dead and under satan's dominance. The devil could exert his authority over you, but that is where his reign stopped, because above him were the angels and above the angels were the spirits of new creatures in CHRIST, seated at the right hand of GOD.

The Hierarchical Order of Spirits in the Spirit Realm

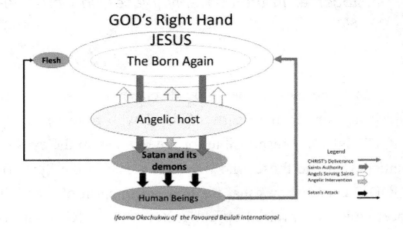

Ifeoma Okechukwu of the Favoured Beulah International

As soon as you get born again, you are translated, from under satan (who is the prince of the kingdom of darkness) into the glorious light of the kingdom of the LORD JESUS CHRIST (Colossians 1:13). You get raised together with CHRIST to the right hand of GOD above angels, satan and the unbelievers. Consequently, as a born again Christian, you were raised with CHRIST, and are presently seated together with Him at the right hand of GOD (Ephesians 2:6). Praise the LORD!

The Spirit of CHRIST is one with our spirits and when HE speaks through your mind that is already renewed, you come through as the actual speaker.

The Mindset of the Righteous

As I have said earlier, a change of mindset is required for anyone who wants to become effective in a new position, be it in a cultural, social or professional status.

In the same way, as a Christian who is determined to operate successfully in the realm of the spirit, you require a change of your mindset. You need to become spiritual in your evaluation of all that concerns you and happens to you. Being born again in the image and likeness of GOD, you are set to operate in your default mode, but because you had already grown up in the world that is tainted with human and unscriptural belief systems, you are at first challenged with the responses of your new nature and are baffled about how to operate in it.

Firstly, you have to become responsive to your spirit, though it feels so new and different. You would immediately notice that your natural desires are changing for spiritual ones. Instead of feeling at home with sinful habits, you begin to dislike and even detest them. Your inclinations now tend towards GOD and spiritual things.

Secondly, you have to realize that these new feelings that tend to focus on GOD and HIS Word, should be nourished, encouraged and even pursued (1 Peter 2:2-3; Matthew 4:4; Luke 4:4: Colossians 3:1-4). You have to deliberately "press forward," focus on them and pursue them, so that they would settle and take root in your spirit (Philippians 3:13-14). There is a need to consciously educate your mind under the leadership of your born-again spirit. You must realize that although, you are a spirit, you live in a body and you have a soul (will, mind, intellect, emotion, feelings and conscience).

Also, your soul and body tend to overpower or overrule your spirit in decision making, and in taking some actions. You may also observe that your spirit is usually stifled under the weight of your soul and body, even when it is contrary to what your spirit desires. That is why you cannot afford to abandon to chance the feeding of your mind with the food of the spirit (Matthew 4:4; Luke 4:4), which is the word of GOD. Understand that though you are in this world, you don't belong to it (John 18:36; 8:23). The domain where you now belong is not of this world (John 8:23). Hence, you should consciously desist from existing in this present world as a permanent resident, and live like a citizen of the spiritual kingdom of the sons of GOD (John 17:16), who is on transit in the present world. Remember that you are only an ambassador on this earth for the purpose of giving out the "word of reconciliation" (reconciling the world to GOD) (2 Corinthians 5: 19-20).

Remember that you are only an ambassador on this earth for the purpose of giving out the "word of reconciliation" (reconciling the world to GOD)

John 17:16 (NKJV)

"They are not of the world, just as I am not of the world."

Thirdly, you should realize that you are not of this world and your ways and manner of reasoning need to change. It is important that you adequately analyze things from two perspectives – the spiritual and the natural. Nothing happens **You are not of this world**
by accident. It is very important to know that you are a spirit and to embrace your spirituality as well as your humanity, because you need your humanity to operate in the physical world, but your worst and most prevalent enemy on earth is satan, a spirit being.

For instance, you may suddenly notice that someone despises you for no reason at all, while another shows you love and favor, practically out of the blue. Situations like these require critical spiritual analysis. If you consider the former case and discover that there is no earthly reason for the resentment, you may have to look at the situation from the realm of the spirit, where natural, human reasoning will not suffice. Thus, you must address the situation from your superior standpoint, the spirit realm. This is the reality of the dual existence of the believer in CHRIST. The Bible shows in 1 Corinthians 2:14 the two perspectives: the spiritual and the natural.

1 Corinthians 2:14-15 (NKJV)

14 "But the natural man does not receive the things of the Spirit of God, for they are foolishness to him; nor can he know them, because they are spiritually discerned. 15 But he who is spiritual judges all things, yet he himself is [rightly] judged by no one."

The natural man, in the passage above, refers to the humanistic world view, a view that does not factor in possible spiritual sides to events, situations and circumstances. This view, of course, does not consider GOD or satan. It does not see any relevance of spirits in the physical world. Yet, the writer of Hebrews declares that the things we see (perceive with our five senses) come from the things we don't see.

Hebrews 11:3 (NKJV)

By faith we understand that the worlds were framed by the word of God, so that the things which are seen were not made of things which are visible [to the five senses of feel, taste, smell, hear, and see]. Parenthesis mine.

Stay on your assigned post because the power behind your commission is omnipotent, omniscient and omnipresent;

Acquiring and maintaining "I am a spirit" mindset, keeps you going forward in the face of difficulties. It makes you stay on your assigned post because the power behind your commission is omnipotent, omniscient and omnipresent; HE has not recalled you from your assignment. Standing firm in the face of difficulties makes you stronger, as your spirit "muscles" get stronger, to win the next battle (Hebrews 5:14b; Ephesians 6:13). That's the gospel truth. That is what the Word says!

You have the power of Christ in Your Spirit

Ephesians 1:19 says that the power that resides in your born-again spirit, works in direct proportion to the mighty power of GOD that raised JESUS from the dead. The Apostle John emphasized the same point when he said that "as CHRIST is, so are you in this world," that is, in your spirit man (1 John 4:17b). The implications include the fact that you have changed from the mindset of a victim to that of a victor: "I (with CHRIST) am in charge." The actions you take need to reflect your spiritual mindset. Salvation guarantees you heaven, but on your way to heaven, it does not guarantee you success in maintaining the victory that JESUS gave you. You must exercise your authority over the devil; and your victory is already guaranteed (Mark 16:17-18; Luke 10:19; etc.).

Curry Blake (the General Overseer of John G. Lake Ministries) says, "Salvation guarantees you heaven but does not guarantee that you would not go through hell on your way to heaven." However, operating as a born again spirit will! Praise be to JESUS CHRIST!

Exercise Your Authority to Maintain Victory

James 4:7 (KJV)

*"Submit yourselves therefore to God. **Resist the devil, and he will flee from you.**"*

Without actively resisting and putting the devil in his place, with all his activities, you will not be very successful in enforcing the word of GOD on your situations and in your life. The scripture clearly guarantees you success in fending off the devil when you resist him.

Without exercising your spiritual authority, you will "go through hell on your way to heaven." The problems and pains of this world have challenged the most brilliant minds, science, and the religious world. Many atheists often use this idea as a crutch for their atheism, which is built on a limited view of the world, its origin and its composition.

I cannot expound on the problem of pain in this book, but I want to point out, that when the right questions about pain are asked, the sincere exploration of the problem would reveal the precise truth that the atheists are afraid of acknowledging, which is GOD. Again, I would like to state that salvation does not exclude

Salvation does not exclude you from the battles of life, the attacks of the devil, sicknesses, diseases, pain, fiery attacks from people or your enemies.

you from the battles of life, the attacks of the devil, sicknesses, diseases, pain, fiery attacks from people or your enemies. It does not guarantee you the manifestations of the love, joy, peace, and so forth; things that you have by the SPIRIT of GOD, but it empowers you to manifest them

Acknowledging what you have in CHRIST, and using it by exercising your spiritual authority gives you the advantage of manifesting less pain and more joy and peace than unbelievers

through CHRIST, because they are all yours in the spirit realm. Acknowledging what you have in CHRIST, and using it by exercising your spiritual authority gives you the advantage of manifesting less pain and more joy and peace than unbelievers (Philemon 1:6).

As it is in the physical realm, you can develop a reputation in the spiritual realm as one that does not take "No" for an answer. When that reputation starts to precede you in every battle, demons would be on the run even before you do or say anything (Acts 19:15). Being a person of your word is more important in the spiritual realm than in the physical. Develop a reputation of saying what you mean and meaning what you say (Psalm 15: 4).

Psalms 15:4 (NLT)

Those who despise flagrant sinners, and honor the faithful followers of the LORD, and keep their promises even when it hurts.

Maintain a connection with the HOLY SPIRIT through

prayer and the study of the Word. These would help in edifying yourself (1 Corinthians 14:3 & Jude 1:20). Start with **your prayer life.** Prayer, here, is not necessarily for you, but for other people, for your country and others as well. Spending quality time with GOD not necessarily asking for things and praying for others enhance your spiritual mindset.

> *1Corinthians 14:4 (NKJV)*
>
> *"He who speaks in a tongue edifies himself, but he who prophesies edifies the church."*
>
> *1 Timothy 2:1 (NKJV)*
>
> *Therefore, I exhort first of all that supplications, prayers, intercessions and giving of thanks be made for all men.*

Insist on creating a Spirit-charged atmosphere around you, always; as often as it depends on you. Do not allow others to occupy, overshadow or take over your spiritual space by changing the atmosphere to what they would rather have. For instance, you could have people who insist on talking about their ideologies, favorite movies, food, games, teams, political affiliations and personalities; and you just sit back and allow them to encroach. By allowing that, you are stifling the real you. Participate in wholesome conversations and be sure to noticeably reject profane talks. Insist on talking about your GOD

Insist on talking about your GOD and CHRIST as often as you have the opportunity. Choose to honor GOD rather than man

and CHRIST as often as you have the opportunity. Choose to honor GOD rather than man (John 5:44). Yes, you will lose some "friends", but you have GOD in your corner. It is all about seeking GOD's honor.

John 5:44 (NKJV)

*"How can you believe, who receive honor from one another, and do not **seek the honor that comes from the only God?"***

The things your family members and friends love to talk about when they are around you are their gods. Those are the things they do when you are in the church or at home worshiping your GOD. Give them audience if necessary, but be quick to talk about your GOD.

For example, "Yeah, I did watch the game after I came back from church on Sunday, but let me tell you something that our Pastor said in his preaching that has stuck with me since Sunday...." Then you can go on to share.

One of two things could happen: they may not have expected you to talk about JESUS but they would listen because you listened to them talk about what they like. On the other hand, they may not like it and may walk away. That would mean that the next time, they will not sit beside you in the cafeteria or staff room, neither will they hang out in your office because they are sure you will mention JESUS CHRIST and HIM crucified!

However, if for any reason they do come, then they already know what they will get from you if they stay by you.

You cannot successfully be a secret agent for JESUS and be a victorious Christian. Many Christians have taken the position of secret agents for CHRIST; they have misinterpreted and misquoted many scriptures about love and living in peace with our neighbors. In their skewed interpretation, they allow their neighbors to charge the atmosphere with profanity and ungodly conversations and conduct, while they just sit and take the trash even when it hurts their spirits badly. Some believe that they are showing love by allowing the unbelievers "be themselves" by abusing them spiritually; yet these Christians hope that their silence and tolerance of their friends' ungodly ways would somehow bring them to CHRIST. Think again. Many of them despise the GOD you love so much! They may either make you to quietly renounce GOD or make you so uncomfortable that you may finally renounce CHRIST.

> **You cannot successfully be a secret agent for JESUS and be a victorious Christian.**

There are two truths that you must know and arm yourself with:

1. No man can come to GOD except HE, GOD, draws him unto HIMSELF.

John 6:65 (NKJV)

"And He said, 'Therefore I have said to you that no one can come to me unless it has been granted to him by My Father.'"

2. You are stifling your spirit and becoming less effective in who you are as a spirit. Every unchallenged abuse of your spirit negatively impacts your reputation in the realm of the spirit. Eventually, if the abuse of your spiritual space is allowed to continue unchallenged, your faith in GOD becomes weaker and weaker untill you find yourself acting more from your flesh (which cannot please GOD) than from your spirit man.

Romans 8:8 (NKJV)

"So then, those who are in the flesh cannot please God."

Therefore, my dear brothers and sisters, silence is not a strategy for spiritual growth. Note that we were born again by the incorruptible Word of GOD and the Gospel is the power of GOD unto salvation. It has to be vocalized to be heard. If you cannot create an atmosphere where the gospel can easily be preached to any of the people you tend to defer to at home, at work, at school,

Silence is not a strategy for spiritual growth.

in the market place, at the Gym, at the game, at the movie theater; then it is very unlikely that you can impress them about GOD by your passivity.

A spiritual mindset would help you to see NO LIM-ITATIONS in changing things around you in your favor. Let me share experience.

After I was born again, I made the decision to go to the church where I worshipped, to pray for at least one hour before every church service. Then, GOD started speaking to me about the church, as a whole, specific individuals and certain events in the church. Some of the Pastors believed me when I shared what GOD told me and some didn't. However, to the best of my knowledge, more than 95% of everything GOD had told me later came to pass.

It is an awesome privilege that sometimes I would see or hear things about individuals in the church or just concerning the church and I always did reverence the GOD that let me into some of the secrets. So I shared them with only the relevant people.

It was a spiritual gift of the discerning of spirits (1 Corinthians 12:10) and I was operating in it for the benefit of the church. All the spiritual gifts listed in 1 Corinthians 12, Ephesians 4:11, Romans 12, and many other gifts in the Bible are essential for the effectiveness of the church of JESUS CHRIST in advancing the kingdom of GOD. As a Christian, you should desire to manifest some of these gifts as they are needed in your local church. The discerning of spirits can particularly be essential in the present era of satan who "transforms himself into an angel of light" (2 Corinthians 11:14).

Live as a Spirit

The emphasis of this chapter is on the fact that you are a spirit and that acknowledging it, embracing it and acting more from your spirit than your flesh, would lead to:

1. Manifest your superiority in CHRIST.

2. It will help you to reach beyond the natural to access spiritual tools that would help you overcome the obstacles and barriers to your victory.

3. It will make you a spiritually available vessel to be used of GOD, to accomplish HIS purpose in anyone, anywhere, across the globe. This would be realized with you, just sitting and talking to HIM in your prayer closet.

4. It will help to keep you always available and always ready, so:

    •   You must become intentional in maintaining the consciousness of your spirituality.

    •   Do not allow any shared public space be dominated by foul and ungodly language or conduct that offends your spirit.

- Spiritually assess everything and everyone more comprehensively, then use spiritual strategies to craft solutions from the spirit realm.

CHAPTER 5

SPIRITUAL CONTEST

Ephesians 6:10-12 (KJV)

*10 "Finally, my brethren, be **strong** in the Lord, and in the power of his might.*

*11 Put on the whole armor of God that ye may be able to stand against the **wiles** of the devil.*

*12 For we **wrestle** not against flesh and blood, but against principalities, against powers, against the rulers of the darkness of this world, against spiritual wickedness in high places."*

This passage is used by most people who teach on spiritual authority to illustrate casting out devils. If you noticed, in the previous chapters, I have not conferred this teachings to casting out demonic forces only. I reiterated the fact that we are blessed and sometimes these blessings just don't manifest physically in our lives; but as a Christian, you have the authority to enforce or cause those blessings to be activated in your life. It is also a call for being strong in the LORD and in the power of HIS might, which literally means that Christians should firmly depend on or have confidence in the LORD and HIS power.

The Passion Translation highlights the supernatural implications of being strong in the LORD as: *"Be supernaturally infused with strength through your life-union with the Lord Jesus. Stand victorious with the force of His explosive power flowing in and through you"* (Ephesians 6:10).

Become GOD Dependent

This point needs to be emphasized because, very often, Christians do not talk to GOD about issues they consider trivial, until things get out of hand, and they are frustrated, not getting their desired solutions. Ephesians 6:10 indicates that our victory is in GOD and in the power of HIS might. Of course, there are many things you can do with the ability GOD has given you without special guidance and directions from HIM. However, taking advantage of HIS strength can only help and not hurt. Jeremiah 10:23 states that GOD did not leave us with exclusive rights to direct our own steps. Thus, standing strong in HIM, is a sure way to give HIM permission to guide and direct you. Besides, the HOLY SPIRIT is given to us also to teach, guide and lead us in our daily walk (John 14:26). Developing and maintaining a mindset that you are a spirit being should lead you to being more GOD-dependent than being more focused on your human abilities and resources.

Verse 11 of the passage above admonishes us to put on all the defensive armory that GOD gave us for the purpose of withstanding the "wiles" of the devil, rather than the power or authority of the devil. The choice of word "wiles" connotes the fact that satan has no official power or authority but uses "wiles" or deceptions against the children of GOD.

According to *Strong's Concordance*, "wiles" which is "meth-od-i'-ah" in Greek, means "travelling over, i.e. travesty (trickery):—wile, lie in wait." In other words, the devil lies in wait with trickery and travesty. Satan is the master of deception and that is mostly what he uses to attack the children of GOD. The most dangerous aspect of deception is that the person being deceived does not even realize it.

> **The most dangerous aspect of deception is that the person being deceived does not even realize it.**

Stick to the Scriptures to Detect Deception

Some of us may be wondering how they may know when they are being deceived. The truth is that on your own, without the right information or the power of the HOLY SPIRIT, you may not know; that is why it is called deception. If you have encountered and tried to change the mind of a deceived person, you would observe that they usually, sincerely argue their position as the truth, even though you know they are wrong. The moment they find out the truth, their deception disappears.

The possibility of being deceived highlights another important reason you should insist on being strong in the LORD and allowing HIM to direct your steps. Whenever applicable, stick to the scriptures and you cannot miss your way.

A Continuous Fight Against Satan

In verse 12, the Bible says that we do not wrestle against human beings; but rather, against the ranks and files of demonic spirits.

> *12 "For we **wrestle** not against flesh and blood, but against principalities, against powers, against the rulers of the darkness of this world, against spiritual wickedness in high places" (Ephesians 6:12).*

The word "wrestle" is another interesting word choice. It is described as the continuous struggle of the Christian to combat the power of evil. The word "**wrestling**" in the *Strong's Concordance* definition, is derived from "**pale**" in Greek, from the root word "**pallo**", which means to "**vibrate**".

"**Pale,**" which is translated "**wrestling**" is used only once in the entire New Testament and it means "a contest between two in which each person endeavors to throw the other, or when the victor is able to hold his opponent down with his hand upon his neck." The term is transferred to the Christian's struggle with the power of evil" (*Strong's Concordance*). This is synonymous with the constant struggle between Christians and the demonic world. We don't back down, we don't standby, but keep wrestling, actively fighting until we have total victory in a particular issue (James 4:7).

Struggling means contesting for what is yours. This is always satan's target and the term is transferred to the Christian's struggle or striving with the power of evil to achieve or maintain something, in the face of difficulties that tend to influence our circumstances or situations, including our relationships and other spiritual activities. Thus, satan tends

> The good news is that the fight is fixed. It doesn't matter how many times the devil comes; as long as you remember who you are, WHOSE you are, and use your authority over him and his demons, you will always emerge the winner.

to follow craftily and frame devices to deceive the children of GOD. The devil succeeded in beating Adam and Eve once; he has tasted the authority GOD gave man and until he is finally sent to the abyss, he will continue to go to and fro, lie in wait, looking for whom he may devour (1 Peter 5:8). Insist on not being his next punching bag. The good news is that the fight is fixed. It doesn't matter how many times the devil comes; as long as you remember who you are, WHOSE you are, and use your authority over him and his demons, you will always emerge the winner.

1 Peter 5:8 (NKJV)

"Be sober, be vigilant; because your adversary the devil walks about like a roaring lion, seeking whom he may devour."

2 Corinthians 2:14 (NKJV)

"Now thanks [be] to God who always leads us in triumph in Christ, and through us diffuses the fragrance of His knowledge in every place."

1 Corinthians 15:57 (NKJV)

"But thanks [be] to God, who gives us the victory through our Lord Jesus Christ."

Your Spouse, Family Members, Friends, Boss, Colleagues are Not the Problem

Referring again to Verse 12, we see that "we wrestle not against flesh and blood." This means that all our struggles are not against our fellow human beings but the wicked spirits. This scripture is literally saying that the fight between you and your spouse, children, or any other person did not originate from that individual but from satan. Many Christians know this scripture but do not refer to it in resolving their disagreements. The tendency often is for Christians to pounce on the "flesh and blood" whom the devil has influenced to be in conflict with them.

Think for a second, of a world where Christians believe this scripture, accept it as their mode of response to conflicts: that would mean close to zero fights between believers. It means that spouses would team up to fight the culprit, friends would team up, and brethren in the church would team up to fight their common enemy – the devil.

Furthermore, Ephesians 2:2-3 also tells us that every none Christian (none born again) acts under the influence of satan. When the "wrestling" is with unbelievers, you should be even more determined to exercise your authority to bind the enemy who is at work in them (Matthew 18:18; Mark 16:17). When you need to settle issues, it is advisable to take authority over the demonic spirits responsible for the conflict, before physically resolving the problem. This would be more effective, and victory would always be guaranteed (Romans 8:37).

Often, while Christians are resolving their conflicts using the natural humanistic approach, the devil takes advantage of their ignorance and continues to perpetrate his evil. Carnal Christians usually focus on the physical manifestations of the enemy, manifested through whoever allows himself to be used of the devil to create or perpetrate the evil.

Imagine this scenario: a husband comes home to his wife, maybe after a tough, stressful day at work. Rather than welcome him, for no discernible reason, his wife attacks him, spoiling for a fight. He tries to backtrack to find out what the problem is, but she raises a tantrum and refuses to communicate coherently. What does the husband do in such a situation? Does he harness his own abusive, quarrelsome skills and give back to his wife in full measure, accusing her of being stupid and unreasonable? Or does he use our approach, as explained in this book?

How great it could be if such a husband, being spiritually wise and sound, retraces his footsteps, probably gets into the room and settles the score with the source of the problem! Such a husband can quietly use his authority to rebuke the devil and run him out of his home, before going back to his wife to settle things. That would work, every time!

With your children, family members, friends, colleagues at work and your boss, you can bind the evil spirit behind the conflicts before physically meeting to discuss and resolve the issue. This two-step approach of binding the devil behind your quarrels first, then scheduling the conflict resolution talk, is the way to arrive at a better and faster conflict resolution. This approach really calls for being conscious of who you are in the spirit realm, knowing that everything that happens to you tends to have a spiritual dimension to it. Remember, don't give satan any place in your life (Ephesians 4:27)

Satan Uses People to Attack You in the Spirit Realm

You are a spirit, and the devil knows and recognizes you in the spirit, but can't fight you in the spirit, because you are higher in the spiritual hierarchy and more powerful than he can ever be (Ephesians 2:6). So, the demons come in the physical realm to seek opportunities to attack. Since they, like GOD, are spirits they need physical bodies to perpetrate their evil plans, so they look for someone with the predisposition for their deceptions, and use them against their fellow human beings.

Don't get me wrong. Because of differences of opinion, likes, dislikes and diversity of taste, people are bound to differ. However, in sorting out your differences, all acts of vilifying one another for their differences, are from the devil. Being spiritual means assessing the disagreements and recognizing that the real enemy is the devil and not the human being. This is what Paul encourages Christians to do, in the passage.

Sometime in 2017, a group of my colleagues ganged up against me and gave our boss an inaccurate, damaging report about me. At the next staff meeting, this group of six were completing one another's sentences in their verbal presentation of an incident that had previously happened. Earlier that day, when GOD showed me about a gang-up against me, I had taken my time to address it in the realm of the spirit, by using my GOD-given authority. Our boss believed the accusations levelled against me, but was interrupted by a senior colleague who came to my defense. Having perfect knowledge of the issue, she stated that if she were in my shoes, she would not have done anything differently from the way I handled it.

"Based on what actually happened," Cheryl continued, "Ifeoma did not do anything wrong." (Cheryl is not her real name).

When next our boss spoke, her tone and demeanor had changed and the blame was directed rightly to where it belonged. On my way back to my office after the meeting, I thanked and worshiped the LORD again. I thanked GOD earlier that day, I had prayed and taken authority over every plan and purpose of the enemy against me. At that meeting, satan was defeated yet again in my life! Praise the LORD!

I remember another incident that happened during my Bible School days. As I got home on a certain day after evangelism, my first son approached me and informed me that I had a visitor, a relative of mine. I got into the living room and met a lady that I had never seen or met before, not even in my wildest imagination. Instantly, I heard in my spirit "steal, kill, and destroy," meaning the lady was not who she claimed to be.

I went into my closet, bowed my head and prayed and

GOD told me what to do: "Feed her and send her away." This was a big temptation because I have a soft spot for little children and pregnant women, and she had a little boy with her; but GOD is wiser and I was determined to obey HIM. By the time we finished dinner it was about 8 p.m. I took them to a half-way house (a temporary shelter for the homeless) and luckily, I knew of one around, and paid for their stay.

The question is: how did she know me? She only knew me from the spirit, because she told me so many things about me, and every single thing she said was like reading my mails to me. She was accurate. However, according to her, she did not know me (physically), and she was not even from Nigeria; she lied to my son to gain access into my home.

However, I wasn't carried away, because demons of darkness can disguise as angels of light. Frankly, if I hadn't spoken with God, I wouldn't have been safe. The devil is a spirit and needs a body to operate from. Moreover, the woman was operating with a witchcraft spirit, because at a point she started confessing. The next morning, the lady and her son were gone from the halfway-house, and nobody knew when they left. I can't stress enough the fact that operating with a spiritual mindset gives you a great advantage and the GOD-given access to spiritual strategies on how things, which started in the spiritual can be resolved in the physical realm.

Areas where the enemy fights Christians

The second implication of the believer's spiritual authority is that every circumstance, situation and activity of spirits can be made to conform to the obedience of the word of GOD.

According to the *Bible Commentary* by Andrew Wommack: "Spiritual wickedness in high places (sometimes referred to as wicked spirits in the earth's atmosphere) is the most frequently engaged enemy that we deal with. The purpose of these spirits is to work against and destroy all that is of Jesus Christ."

They do this in the following ways:

1. Hindering God's work :(1Thessalonians 2:17-18, Acts 17:1-9, Luke 4:5-6, and Revelation 2:10):

As a team leader of an evangelical effort to preach the gospel on the streets of Detroit, I usually encouraged my team members to be aware of possible hindrances to their

Insist on moving forward in the face of the challenge.

decision to work for GOD. At every point in time, your decision to do the work of GOD will be challenged, but if you stand your ground and keep going, even when it seems impossible to do so, you will win. The only way to know that it is not impossible is to insist on moving forward in the face of the challenge. For example, every member of my team had the option to commit to at least one Saturday in a month. However, I told them that their commitment needed to be a decision that is set in stone, one that could not falter even if keeping that commitment hurt.

Headache, stomach ache, conflict in the home, and so forth, would emerge either on Friday evenings or on the Saturdays of their choice – the goal being to stop them from going out to evangelize. My personal experience was that, whatever the enemy planned to use to stop me usually disappeared, as soon as I stepped out of the house to fulfill my commitment. That was how I knew it was specifically meant to stop the work of GOD.

Church leaders and ministers of GOD all over the world face several kinds of attacks from the enemy because they are snatching people out of the kingdom of darkness. JESUS said that there would be persecution and afflictions, for the word's sake.

Mark 4:17 (NKJV)

"and they have no root in themselves, and so endure only for a time. Afterward, when tribulation or persecution arises for the word's sake, immediately they stumble."

According to JESUS, tribulation and persecution arise for the word's sake. When a Christian makes the decision to stand on or do the word of GOD, they should not be surprised to experience tribulation and persecution. Satan prevented Paul and Silas from following up the Christians in Thessalonica and their host, Jason was beaten up for hosting Paul and Silas (1 Thessalonians 2:17-18, Acts 17:1-9). JESUS was tempted not to fulfill the work of GOD for which HE came (Luke 4:5-6). In a prophecy to the church in Smyrna, the Apostle John encouraged them not to be shaken by the attacks of the devil: *"Don't be afraid of what you are about to suffer. The devil will throw some of you into prison to test you. You will suffer for days. But if you remain faithful even when facing death, I will give you the crown of life" (Revelation 2:10 NLT).*

2. Blinding the minds of people (2 Corinthians 4:4).

Satan was attributed with the ability to blind people's minds, which could mean deceiving them, so that they would not see the value of, and hence receive the gospel of JESUS; and ultimately, they would not have the light of GOD shine in their hearts.

2 Corinthians 4:4 (NLT)

*"**Satan**, who is the god of this world, has **blinded the minds** of those who don't believe. They are **unable to see the glorious light of the***

*Good News. They don't understand this mes-
sage about the glory of Christ, who is the exact
likeness of God."*

In 2 Corinthians 4:4, we are told that the goal of satan
is blinding the eyes of his captives so that they are not able
to see the light of the gospel. Although the word "blind" in
Strong's Concordance means "inability to see physically,"
it is used here in a more metaphorical than literal sense.
It means, "to blunt the mental discernment, darken the
mind… to obscure."

The devil, literally, is the one responsible for blinding
unbelievers from seeing and accepting the good news of
the cross. The humanistic approach of assessing and explaining away everything in life, can be attributed to the
activity of satan blinding the eyes of the proponents of all
such viewpoints, believers inclusive. All forms of the "…
Jews requesting a sign, and Greeks seeking after wisdom,"
(1 Corinthians 1:22 (NKJV)), together form the humanism
that always stands against spiritual viewpoints. Based on
this, you can pray that GOD would remove blinders off the
eyes of your loved ones.

3. Beguiling, misleading, and deceiving people (2
Corinthians 11:3).

Beguiling, is a situation where the reason you believe
you are doing something is different from the real reason

for which that thing exists. There are many such political issues today. One of the first originators of the legalization of abortion in the United States, proposed it as a means for "race cleansing", (https://www.americanheritage.com/race-cleansing-america), that is, weeding off impure races and atypical human beings. Margaret Sanger, in her 1920s Birth Control Review publications, was clear about her philosophy of human life, and with deceptions in the quote below, she was able to push through her eugenics agenda.

"We do not want word to go out that we want to exterminate the Negro population and the minister is the man who can straighten out that idea if it ever occurs to any of their more rebellious members." ~Letter from Margaret Sanger to Dr. C.J. Gamble, December 10th, 1939.

However, overtime, it metamorphosed and was sold to Americans as issues of women's health and for rape cases. This was a more palatable reason to perpetrate such evil.

As Christians, who know that we are spirits and that satan is always looking for ways to blind, beguile and mislead by deception, it is important for us to know what we are signing up for, when we support something like abortion or organizations which push policies that contradict who we are in the spirit. In all, satan's goal is to kill, steal and destroy (John 10:10), through deceptive devices that make people *"live by whatever natural cravings and thoughts their minds dictate, living as rebellious children who are subject to GOD's wrath" (Ephesians 2:3 TPT).* On the other hand, know that JESUS has ensured by HIS sacrifice, that we don't become prisoners of self-defeating patterns of behavior.

4. Tempting people (1 Corinthians 7:5).

Satan literally lies in wait, looking for opportunities and who, to tempt. For the Christian, the need to be vigilant cannot be over emphasized. The battle ground is usually the mind of human beings, but the weapons of GOD, which are powerful through GOD, is available to all of us that are born again (2 Corinthians 10:3-5).

5. Buffeting GOD's people (2 Corinthians 12:7).

Satan takes advantage of Christians' weaknesses to attack them. He is the master of coordinated attacks. For instance, the day your spouse is acting up, is the day your children disturb you the most. The day your boss at work is losing her mind and blaming it on you, is the same day you commit a seemingly irreparable blunder with your friend and for some reason, your paycheck is delayed. You may want to scream at the top of your voice or anything else your carnal tendencies dictate, but cursing GOD cannot be an option, because that is exactly what the devil wants you to do.

One way to be able to stand with a smile on your face and gratitude in your heart, is to thank GOD for all your problems and remember that GOD, who brought you out in the past, would surely do it again. HE is still GOD, the One who loves you above everyone else including yourself. HE will deliver you! Besides, you are in charge, to enforce obedience on satan and his demons, asking them to leave, and they will!

Remembering to adequately address coordinated attacks of the devil as described above comes mostly by being and acting from your spirit, thinking spiritually more than carnally. Responding reflexively as a spirit being stems from practice, and the more you practice being spiritual, the more reflexively you will respond, and victories will come.

6. Attempting to corrupt and infiltrate the church of JESUS CHRIST (2 Corinthians 11:15 and 1 Timothy 4:1).

Another way the devil wrestles against children of GOD, is by attempting to corrupt and infiltrate the church. Usually the goal here, is to create distractions, confusion and conflicts, both on a personal and at church levels, by perpetrating all kinds of hindrances with the leadership and the congregants. The church is open to everyone and many different kinds of people come in; both those who mean well and those who don't.

You are more likely to be discerning of people's spirits if you are sensitive to the Spirit of GOD, and if you are praying for your church. GOD's gift to the church: apostles, prophets, evangelists, pastors and teachers, serve different purposes in the church. Everyone else can help the pastor by praying for the local church not to be saddled with "wrong" people in the highest or sensitive positions. If you consider a church as yours, then you must pray for that church, as anything that goes wrong in it can also affect you.

Maintaining Victory in exercising Spiritual Authority.

7. First, control your emotions: Don't get upset very easily. Negative emotions are typical examples of the humanistic approach to GOD. Don't war after the flesh (2 Corinthians 10:3-5).

Don't war after the flesh

2 Corinthians 10:3-5.

*"**For although we live in the natural realm, we don't wage a military campaign employing human weapons,** using manipulation to achieve our aims. **Instead, our spiritual weapons are energized with divine power to effectively dismantle the defenses behind which people hide. We can demolish every deceptive fantasy[e] that opposes God and break through every arrogant attitude that is raised up in defiance of the true knowledge of God.** We capture, like prisoners of war, every thought and insist that it bows in obedi-*

ence to the Anointed One."

8. Keep watch! Pay attention (2 Corinthians 10:6).

1 Corinthians 10:6

*"Since we are armed with such dynamic weaponry, we **stand ready to punish any trace of rebellion,** as soon as you choose complete obedience."*

In the above scripture and many others, believers are admonished to "watch", especially so that the devil does not get us unaware and unprepared (1 Peter 4:7; 2 Timothy 4:5; 1 Thessalonians 5:6).

9. Don't be presumptuous.

Don't assume that the devil cannot use you, the Bible teacher. Consider the following scriptures:

1 Corinthians 16:13 (KJV)

"Watch ye, stand fast in the faith, quit you like men, be strong."

Colossians 4:2 (KJV)

"Continue in prayer, and watch in the same with thanksgiving."

1 John 4:1 (KJV)

"Beloved, believe not every spirit, but try the spirits whether they are of God: because many false prophets are gone out into the world."

1 Thessalonians 5:21 (KJV)

"Prove all things; hold fast that which is good."

10. Travel light: Don't be entangled with weights that could drag you down.

Don't be entangled with weights that could drag you down.

Don't get too busy; don't have too many things going on.

2 Timothy 2:3, 4 (KJV)

3 "Thou therefore endure hardness, as a good soldier of Jesus Christ.

4 No man that warreth entangleth himself with the affairs of [this] life; that he may please him who hath chosen him to be a soldier."

CHAPTER 6
INTIMACY WITH GOD

The central theme of the entire Bible is GOD becoming man on earth for the singular purpose of securing the salvation of man, so that man would fulfill HIS purpose on the earth. The events associated with the Old Testament presents a perspective of GOD and HIS mode of operations before JESUS CHRIST came on the scene, revealing and preserving key elements that were the precursors to the ultimate delivery of the salvation of man, which is the main event of the New Testament. GOD is love and this was the motivator of GOD'S benevolence in the salvation of man (1 John 4:8-21). Consequently, love has become the only acceptable motivation for all actions in Christian living (1 John 4:29; 1 Corinthians 13:1-8).

GOD offered man reconciliation and the pathway to intimate relationship through JESUS CHRIST (John 3:16, 17:2-3; 2 Corinthians 5:18). Therefore, seeking and growing in intimacy with GOD remains the predominant goal of the Christian walk, as well as the root of all acceptable activities of the Christian (Matthew

22:37-40; Mark 12:29-33; Luke 10:27-28; Romans 13:9-10; Galatians 5:14; James 2:8).

Matthew 22:37-40 (NKJV)

37 "Jesus said to him, 'You shall love the LORD your God with all your heart, with all your soul, and with all your mind.'

38 This is [the] first and great commandment. And [the] second [is] like it: 'You shall love your neighbor as yourself.' On these two commandments hang all the Law and the Prophets."

In 1 Corinthians 1:22-25, we saw that spiritual things cannot be discerned by humanistic wisdom of the human senses; that is, the five-senses-based reasoning (1 Corinthians 2:14). Although Hebrews 11:6 and John 7:17 both offer benefits for seeking GOD and the methodology for proving HIM respectively, intimacy with GOD seems to elude many believers.

The authority given to Christians at the new birth, like the other benefits, manifests more when they increase their intimacy with GOD. GOD does not pick at will or choose to whom HE would extend HIS blessings and gifts. HE has already given all, released all the benefits of the death and resurrection of our LORD JESUS CHRIST to believers in the spiritual/heavenly realm.

At the new birth, the believers are translated from the kingdom of darkness into that kingdom of LIGHT

(Colossians 1:13) where they assume or take possession of "all blessings in heavenly places" (Ephesians 1:3) and "all things that pertain to life and godliness" (2 Peter 1:3). Whether or not they walk in their spiritual authority and other benefits depends on the Christian. This is the privilege of being born again; thus, the believer can utilize and appropriate their blessings and also place restraints on the activities of satan against him and others around him.

Intimacy with GOD remains the most effective way to be more sensitive, alert and aptly respond to and effectively neutralize the activities of the devil. The act of being a Christian culminates in living for GOD and doing all things heartily to the LORD (Colossians 3:23-24).

Colossians 3:23-24 (NKJV

"And whatever you do, do it heartily, as to the Lord and not to men, knowing that from the Lord you will receive the reward of the inheritance; for you serve the Lord Christ."

Intimacy with GOD starts with the act of being born again. Further growth in the Christian life requires growing in that intimacy and ultimately "entering into the rest of GOD" (Hebrews 4:11). Though this may not be obvious as the target of all New Testament doctrine, however, every decision, every intent of the heart, every motivation and the ultimate action of a Christian impacts the subject of intimacy with GOD – negatively or positively. A Christian who never grew in his intimacy with GOD could still go to heaven after his earthly life, but could suffer a lack of fulfillment in GOD, while he is alive. A Christian's final destination after life on earth could also be jeopardized by his continuously living a life that does not depict his belief in JESUS CHRIST (Titus 1:16).

Intimacy with GOD is an effective way of developing confidence in GOD, which could elude a Christian except he pursues it consciously. On the negative side, the lack of it could result in doubting the power of GOD.

Matthew 14:25-30

25 "Now in the fourth watch of the night Jesus went to them, walking on the sea. 26 And when the disciples saw him walking on the sea, they were troubled, saying, 'It is a ghost!' And they cried out for fear.

27 But immediately Jesus spoke to them saying, 'Be of good cheer! It is I, be not afraid.'

28 And Peter answered him and said, 'Lord, if it is you command me to come to you on the water.'

29 So He said, 'Come.' And when Peter had come down from the boat, he walked on the water to go to Jesus.

30 But when he saw that the wind was boisterous, he was afraid; and beginning to sink he cried out, saying, 'Lord save me!'"

Like Peter, when Christians doubt and look down on their spiritual ability, they inadvertently doubt GOD's power to work through them. If they don't use it, they would eventually lose it.

Some years ago, there was a meeting in the town hall, to lay off people from my work place. I told a Christian sister who was by me, that I would not participate because I wouldn't be in the lay-off list because my work at the Organization was not yet done.

My sister-in-the-LORD, who was also my colleague, disdainfully said, "Ifeoma, is there something you know that I don't know?"

"Yes," I said, "GOD brought me here, and HE will tell me when to leave."

She walked away, upset; but she did not understand that I was exercising the spirit of faith, speaking what I believed (2 Corinthians 4:13).

GOD does not have to tell you everything HE is doing, but if you have a vibrant intimate relationship with HIM, HE will NEVER leave you to hang out and dry (Hebrews 13:5; Isaiah 54:4). There is absolutely no problem with GOD and HIS backing you up, but there could be a problem with your confidence in your ability to exercise your authority.

When you study the story of the children of Israel (which is a type and shadow of the Church of GOD) you would notice that GOD was always calling them to live a life separate from the people around them. In this sense, you can be part of an organization and still be a child of GOD. You can be a member of a family where everyone turns against you, and still be a child of GOD. The issue with most Christians is that they want to be like everyone else, as well as, be liked by everyone else. Intimate relationship with GOD gives you a cushion – to be alone in a crowd and not miss the people. Intimacy with GOD would cause you to seek the acceptance and honor of GOD, more than those of men, and this in turn strengthens your confidence in HIM (John 5:44).

John 5:44 (NKJV)

"How can you believe, who receive honor from one another, and do not seek the honor that comes from the only God?"

Lack of confidence is actually a lack of faith in GOD. Believing is not automatic. If you have been living just like every other person, when challenging situations or circumstances arise, you will not be able to automatically exercise faith in GOD to do the impossible; because you prefer approval from men rather than from GOD.

Believing is not automatic.

This can be likened to the trend in the world. Daily,

the world commits all forms of sins and atrocities, without trying to hide it from others, yet Christians are afraid to live righteously among them. There is something definitely wrong with this practice; this means that Christianity has not become a life style for such an individual. It is just something he does, not something he is. GOD has called us to be Christians, not to do Christianity!

Intimacy guarantees closeness with GOD. It means that there is a love relationship between you and GOD. GOD takes it a step further: HE sends the Spirit of JESUS, to dwell in you (Galatians 4:6), and HE seals that union with the HOLY SPIRIT as a deposit of all HIS promises (Ephesians 1:13; 2 Corinthians 1: 22). Then, HE, the SPIRIT abides permanently, residing in you (John 14:16-17, 23, 26). GOD is truly LOVE! Dwelling in a born again spirit is a compliment of the highest order that GOD could have paid the Christian!

John 14:23 (KJV)

"Jesus answered and said unto him, 'If a man love me, he will keep my words: and my Father will love him and we will come unto him, and make our abode with him.'"

The indwelling Spirit of GOD ensures that you have an enriched fellowship with the GOD-head who dwells in you. HE teaches and reminds you of all you need to adequately and promptly exercise your spiritual authority.

Intimacy with GOD has to be a lifestyle

Psalms 15:1-5 (NKJV)

1 "LORD, who may abide in Your tabernacle? Who may dwell in Your holy hill?

2 He who walks uprightly and works righteousness and speaks the truth in his heart.

3 He who does not backbite with his tongue nor does evil to his neighbor, nor does he take reproach against his friend;

4 In whose eye vile person is despised but he honors those who fears the Lord, he whose swears to his own hurt and does not change.

5 He who does not put his own money as usury nor does he take a bribe against the innocent, he who does this things shall never be moved."

The lifestyle of one who doesn't just visit, but permanently resides in GOD and GOD in him, as expressed in Psalm 15 is revealing. For your personal conduct, the following would be expected of you, not so that GOD would love you, but as expressions of your gratitude for HIS Love:

a. To walk uprightly

b. To work righteousness (be drawn to righteous living and desire to live for GOD)

c. To speak the truth in the heart always (no guile, or deceptions)

d. Not to backbite with your tongue

e. Not to commit evil against your neighbor

f. Not to take up a reproach against your friend

g. In your eyes a vile person (a person who hates GOD and GOD's people) is despised

h. To honor those who fear the LORD

i. To keep promises even when it hurts

j. Not to charge interest when lending money to your brethren

k. Not to take a bribe against the innocent

GOD's guarantee is that you "shall never be moved," disappointed or ashamed. A close review of the list above shows that, if Christian values don't show up in every aspect of your life, you will also not remember or live in the consciousness that you should exercise your authority as often as you should. When you study the life of JESUS, you would see that HE grew in wisdom and favor before GOD and man; therefore, HE is a good example for us to emulate. We should strive to grow in intimacy with GOD and HE will definitely direct our paths.

Imagine this challenge: I had to go against the grain, as an employee in a civil and human rights organization, where everyone had been urged to vote for a particular political party. However, I voted otherwise. That decision was not a difficult one for me because due to my relationship with GOD, I had established myself all through my stay in the organization as a Christian first; and my relationship with GOD reflected on my choice of affiliation, whether gender, race, nationality or ideology. I could not engage in a group identity, except that of the body of CHRIST. I stood out as having only one identity – my Christian identity.

Since without controversy, our attitudes and behavior reflect the identity we assume, identifying myself as a believer and proudly wearing the badge of CHRIST increased my confidence in GOD. It established me as "the go-to" person for people who needed GOD's interventions, and provided me ample opportunities to share the love of GOD to many of my colleagues. Although some stayed away from me because of my badge of honor, GOD magnified HIS name in the many miraculous interventions that I enjoyed in that organization.

A lot of people have multiple identities which leave them confused, perplexed, and unable to express who they are in the LORD. As a child or son of GOD (John 1:12; 1 John 3:1; Galatians 3:26; Ephessians 5:1), there is only one identity that you should have and that is: "The son or child of GOD." I am not black or white, neither am I an African nor an American, male nor female (Ephesians 3:28). I'm a member of the heavenly and that is where I live from. I'm not 100% perfect but I operate with the perfect Spirit of GOD.

Testimony about my salvation

After I was convinced that GOD exists, there was no doubt in my mind that I was supposed to live for HIM. Not being very familiar with the Bible and GOD's expectations for the people HE created, I thought HE was the brilliant mind behind the moral laws, which I had grown to admire. During my atheistic years, I thought someone was behind the law of right and wrong, which I believed placed restraints on the powerful from crushing the weak and regulated the survival of the fittest. I spent endless hours in the library seeking and searching for the truth. The Christianity that was introduced to me did not convince me of the existence of GOD. It was presented as a dogma where no questions were allowed whatsoever, and I had many questions.

The elders obliged me and answered all the questions my inquisitive mind could conjure. Some of the answers were not always satisfactory but would generate more series of questions. Most of the elders loved it and were willing to engage with me as long as it took and sometimes they rescheduled for another day. A few thought that I was annoyingly inquisitive and would not bother to humor me, but that did not deter me. My questions ranged from tradi-tional and cultural issues, to controversial topics, like why, culturally, men seemed to mistreat women.

Then I grew old enough to start catechism (a religious training, used by the Catholic Church, to prepare young people or new converts to become eligible to take the Eu-charist, which means the Holy Communion). Catechism involved a pre-set number of classes that you must success-fully complete before becoming certified to partake in the sacrament of Eucharist. There were innumerable opportuni-ties for questions about GOD, HIS nature, HIS disposition: whether HE is wicked or kind, why HE needs a wide range of people in HIS heaven in terms of age, level of education, gender and so on. I thought that if HE made human beings, HE could make a new set in heaven, rather than break the hearts of people on earth by taking their loved ones.

I was almost thrown out of one of the classes once for asking the Rev. Minister (I am not sure if he was a priest or a brother) what was considered a heresy. We had just finished praying the rosary, our Lord's Prayer, and had just gone through a litany of saints praying for us, then he said, "Let us pray."

I asked out, loudly, "What have we been doing all this time, that we are just starting to pray?" I was genuinely con-fused, and I was not trying to be controversial. The teacher got so mad at me that he warned me with a threat to stopped me from completing the class, if I don't "behave properly."

There were other things that drove more nails into the coffin of my disbelief in the existence of GOD, like the hypocrisy that I witnessed, encountered and experienced during my years of searching. However, the unsatisfied intellectual curiosity was the most powerful of all my reasons. My atheism did not start in college but I had a better opportunity to express it and to even write about it on the department's bulletin board.

I am not sure I properly processed any thought of the consequences of the existence of GOD, because I honestly did not believe that GOD exists. Thus, when I became born again, all I knew was that I wanted to spend the rest of my life with HIM and for HIM, not because HE required it of me, but as my own personalized unique choice. Almost immediately after my conversion, I started sharing the love of GOD with everyone who allowed me. I felt an obligation to tell others that GOD, WHOM I had denied HIS existence for the first twenty-eight years of my life, actually exists and that HE Loves me. However, I did not think that they had to make the same commitment that I had in mind; I just told them that HE loved them too.

How I pursued my desire to spend the rest of my life with and for GOD, took different turns. It started by me kneeling down in the middle of my living room and asking GOD to take my life, which HE did. Figuratively, HE did take my life. I know this because, since that day I said, "I do," I have not looked back again. Praise the LORD!

I was born again on February 8, 1986 and went to church the next day, staying there from about 6 a.m. until after 7 p.m. I was so hungry for GOD that I stayed in the church and participated in every service at St. Paul's Catholic Church, on the Sunday after my conversion. The next day, on my way from work, I followed a group of people who were headed to an evening service by Rev. Father Anozie at the Government Boys College, Okigwe Road, Owerri, Nigeria. The school was right by the secondary school where I was a Mathematics teacher at the time. The service was a lot livelier than the regular Catholic service, so I was a lot more expressive in my worship of the LORD than was encouraged in the church I had attended the day before.

After the service, the priest whom I did not know, nor had ever seen me before, shared with me the vision that three of his trusted congregants saw about me. The first thought in my mind, even before I found out the details of the vision, was: "GOD, I am coming to you today." Three of Rev. Anozie congregation saw independently that my feet were not touching the ground but I was surrounded by bright stars, which assumed any shape I made, including when I knelt down to take the Holy Communion.

After the service, I ran back to my apartment, prayed earnestly that GOD should take my life so that I could be with HIM. I was at the best place of my life, at that point in time. I had no pain or regret other than the fact that I should have believed earlier.

Then I opened a brand-new Bible that I had received as a gift at my school earlier that day, and started reading the Book of Ephesians, Chapter One. I was so disappointed when I woke up the next day, but was pleasantly curious about three words, hand written across my brand-new Bible that read: "Now we go." As I prayed and inquired about the meaning of the stars and the hand written words on my Bible, I was led to Psalm 125: 1-2 in general but Verse 2, in particular:

> *Psalms 125:1-2 (NKJV) 1 A Song of Ascents.*
>
> *"Those who trust in the LORD [Are] like Mount Zion, [Which] cannot be moved, [but] abides forever.*
>
> *2 As the mountains surround Jerusalem, So the LORD surrounds His people from this time forth and forever."*

The stars were GOD's protection around me "as we go", that is, as we (GOD and I) embarked on a lifetime journey. It was the highest honor for me to work with and for GOD!

Anything I thought of, said, did or did not do, was targeted at serving the LORD! I did not always do everything right and certainly was far from being perfect, but my heart and my eyes were set on HIM to revere HIM, and to defer to HIM in all things.

I had no name, nor was I conceptually aware of how to characterize my relationship with GOD, but I was indeed pursuing intimacy with my LORD and my GOD. I guess I was so busy pursuing intimacy with HIM, that I did not pay attention to doctrinal issues and formal definitions of some technicalities or Christian words like "faith" and "sin".

Moreover, I exercised faith when I needed to, and lived a sinless life more effortlessly than on purpose. Many times, the meaning of these words or the special classes convened to discuss them held little or no interest for me. Do not get me wrong; those intellectual exercises are important for proper presentation and increased understanding of the gospel. I can arguably claim that the ultimate of all Christian preaching and teaching is to disciple Christians to walk in conformity with the Word of GOD, and in intimacy with GOD. This is what I was already doing and am still craving. The manifestations of HIS blessings or gifts (including authority and power) are incidentals of the relationship. I must add, at this point, that I do not believe that the manifestations of the benefits of the death and the resurrection of our LORD JESUS CHRIST, exhibited in the life of an individual, confirms HIM as being intimate with, or holy, before the LORD.

However, I do believe that the corollary is true. That

is, if you are intimate with GOD, think the right thoughts about HIM, and relate lovingly with HIM, HIS blessings, gifts, authority, and power would manifest in your life naturally. You would not necessarily need special times of prayer and fasting for HIS benefits to flow in your life. They will simply work by grace.

Here is the summary of everything I have shared above, about my conversion experience:

Intimacy with GOD is the most effective way of enjoying all that HE has given you. When GOD becomes the love of your life and you pursue intimacy with HIM with all you've got, every mountain will become small in your eyes. This is because the pursuit of intimacy with GOD makes your eyes single and when that happens, the light that is in you would be greater than every darkness imaginable (Matthew 6:22), and in every situation, GOD will be BIGGER and your problem smaller.

The pursuit of intimacy with GOD would cause you to seek HIS approval only. You would seek to honor HIM and be honored by HIM more than the honor that comes from men. It would inadvertently impact the faith you have in GOD.

JESUS expressed this in John 5:44 when HE told the religious rulers why they could not have faith in HIM. HE told them that they were seeking approval from each other and did not care whether GOD approved of their conduct or not.

John 5:44 (NKJV)

"How can you believe, who receive honor from one another, and do not seek the honor that [comes] from the only God?"

Notice that JESUS was not saying that they did not seek the honor that HE gave, but that they did not exclusively seek HIS honor? Is GOD against honoring you? No! Honoring you is HIS heart's purpose for keeping you here after salvation, so that you can be part of HIS plan to teach satan and his cohorts HIS manifold wisdom (Ephesians 3:10). The Bible is explicit that those who trust GOD shall never be displaced or moved (Psalm 125), because HE will be with them in trouble, deliver them and honor them (Psalm 91:14-15)!

Psalms 125:1-2 (NKJV) A Song of Ascents.

1 "Those who trust in the LORD [Are] like Mount Zion, Which cannot be moved, but abides forever.

2 As the mountains surround Jerusalem, So the LORD surrounds His people From this time forth and forever."

So, HE wants to honor you, and HE has this exclusive right, not necessarily because you serve HIM, but because that's what HE does. It is by faith that it might be by grace (Romans 4:16).

During my PhD class, there were a couple of people who did not care much about me, for two reasons. First, **I was not a closet Christian; everyone knew that I was all about CHRIST.** Secondly, which stems from the first, **I spoke up for the ideologies that I stood for**, which were contrary to the popular opinion.

GOD had guided me, revealed books and articles for me to read and supported me through a group of people. HE used some, more directly than others, to help me with my PhD work.

Three days before my defense, I heard the LORD say, "Be still and know that I am GOD, I will be exalted among the heathen." I went ahead and completed that quotation. When I woke up the next morning, I heard the same thing again, then I knew GOD was about to do something extraordinary, but I was not quite sure at that point what it would be.

At my defense, GOD was exalted! All six, seasoned, internationally famous professors, unanimously confirmed that my research was the best of its kind they had seen yet! GOD was exalted among the heathens! Praise the LORD!

The Peaceful Rest of GOD

Growing in intimacy with GOD, to the point where you enter into the peaceful rest of GOD, is the ultimate state of intimacy. This is a rest based on absolute confidence because you are sure that the deed, whatever it may be, is done and completed. Your authority and other blessings are assured because your heart indicts a good matter and you know that all HE has given you are yours by right and must manifest in your life (Philemon 1:6).

Hebrews 4:1-11 (NKJV

1 "Therefore, since a promise remains of entering His rest, let us fear lest any of you seem to have come short of it.

2 For indeed the gospel was preached to us as well as to them; but the word which they heard did not profit them, not being mixed with faith in those who heard [it.] 3 For we who have believed do enter that rest, as He has said: 'So I swore in My wrath, They shall not enter My rest, although the works were finished from the foundation of the world.

4 For He has spoken in a certain place of the seventh [day] in this way: 'And God rested on the seventh day from all His works;

5 and again in this [place:] 'They shall not enter My rest.'

6 Since therefore it remains that some [must] enter it, and those to whom it was first preached did not enter because of disobedience,

7 again He designates a certain day, saying in David, 'Today,' after such a long time, as it has been said: 'Today, if you will hear His voice, Do not harden your hearts.'

8 For if Joshua had given them rest, then He would not afterward have spoken of another day.

9 There remains therefore a rest for the people of God.

10 For he who has entered His rest has himself also ceased from his works as God [did] from His.

11 Let us therefore be diligent to enter that rest, lest anyone fall according to the same example of disobedience."

Hebrews 4:2 explicitly shows how people manifest the benefits of JESUS CHRIST by mixing the gospel they hear with faith. Having faith is one thing; then, mixing the gospel with faith, sounds like a purely physical phenomenon, a function of the cognitive ability; but nothing could be further from the truth.

Faith is a spiritual phenomenon that manifests with physical evidence, and if spiritual things are spiritually determined, judged or discerned, then how can a carnal man mix faith with the gospel he has heard?

This might sound rhetorical but it actually does take walking with the Spirit of GOD, to serve the LORD. JESUS said that no man can come to HIM except the FA-

THER draws him. GOD gave us the free will to choose to serve HIM, to choose to defer to HIM, and to choose to be guided by HIM. This makes sense, considering that HE warned that man would die if they ate the fruit of the tree of good and evil; man defied HIM and ate it. GOD was not hurt by that act of disobedience but man became incapable of manifesting the image, likeness; the glory and power of GOD. It is ironical that what man thought would make him wiser than (or at least as wise as) GOD, rather became a terrible handicap that prevented him from knowing his future.

I am not suggesting that he had knowledge of the future before the fall, but then, he was wise enough to talk with GOD and defer to GOD as often. Defining for himself right and wrong, a consequence of eating the forbidden fruit from the tree of knowledge of good and evil, with no point of reference, was the origin of atheism. Although, for the first set of human beings, there was GOD, they chose to live as if there was no GOD and the process of the evolution of the sins of man culminated in the notion that there is no GOD. How could there be GOD, if everyone did what was right in their own eyes?

Herein lies that fallacy of theism that encourages life with little or no reference to GOD. If you claim that there is GOD but you are not sure HE wants you to be a believer at your workplace, at the market place, at your home, and everywhere, you have reduced your position to that of an atheist. Outwardly, the outcome of your actions and thought processes are recognizable: the absence of GOD. Since no one can access your heart to verify whether or not you believe in the existence of GOD, this conclusion becomes highly probable. I would want to believe you because you say so, but the outcome contradicts your words.

Philippians 2:12-13 (NKJV)

12 "Therefore, my beloved, as you have always obeyed, not as in my presence only, but now much more in my absence, work out your own salvation with fear and trembling;

13 for it is God who works in you both to will and to do for [His] good pleasure."

After admonishing us to "work out our salvation with fear and trembling," Paul in the above scriptures added that GOD is the one behind all your good thoughts and actions. The New Living Translation says: *"God is working in you, giving you the desire and the power to do what pleases him."* Praise the LORD!

I believe that there is a form of division of labor in our relationship with GOD. Beyond the act of saying Yes to the LORD, by a belief that leads to being born again or getting converted – an act that is also enabled by HIM – our most central role is to pursue intimacy with GOD. After this, every sincere action, geared towards knowing HIM, is rewarded with increased desire to know HIM, as we seek

HIM diligently. One of the many rewards of growing in intimacy with HIM is seeing all your mountains as small, in the light of GOD and HIS power working in us. You become more aware of and have more confidence that the GOD you have grown fond of, is for you and never against you, as you manifest continuous victory over all the wiles of the enemy, because you are in HIM and with HIM. That is faith! At times like this, mixing faith with the Word becomes effortless.

Hebrew 4:3 (KJV)

"Labor to enter into HIS Rest...."

This scripture (laboring to enter into GOD's rest) is addressing the effort you make to seek to know GOD, not laboring to do things that make GOD like you. Performance based relationship is legalistic and negates grace. All that we receives from GOD is by grace. There is need for works that demonstrate that we believe, but our works do not earn us any scores or points with GOD. "Laboring" in Hebrews 4:11 is about steps we take and efforts we make to know GOD more and to grow in intimacy with HIM. This involves every aspect of our lives – mind, will, emotions, feelings, conscience, likes and dislikes. That's what it means to love the LORD our GOD with all our heart, soul, strength and might (Matthew 22:37; Mark 12:30; Luke 10:27).

Pursuing intimacy with GOD is actually being a Christian, rather than doing Christian things. The world has its mode of operation, of which we were part, before we became born again. However, after the grace of GOD that brought salvation has appeared to us, the godly thing to

> **Pursuing intimacy with GOD is actually being a Christian, rather than doing Christian things.**

do in the pursuit of intimacy with the ONE who just married us, is to forsake all else in our loyalty and pursuit of pleasure, and go after HIM with all our heart, soul and strength. We must reject the mold of the world, refuse to fit into it anymore and labor to be Christians indeed.

We have seen GOD's love, mercy and wisdom: how does HE expect us to respond? Paul's letter to the Christians in Rome is an answer for us:

Romans (The Phillips Translation) 12:1-2

"With eyes wide open to the mercies of God, I beg you, my brothers, as an act of intelligent worship, to give him your bodies, as a living sacrifice, consecrated to him and acceptable by him. Don't let the world around you squeeze you into its own mold, but let God re-mold your minds from within, so that you may prove in practice that the plan of God for you is good, meets all his demands and moves towards the goal of true maturity."

The irony of this is that the mold the world has built

and wants Christians to fit into, dampens their effectiveness and renders them irrelevant in the world. When Christians become powerless and ineffective, the world around them takes pleasure in announcing their use-lessness and then seeks to eliminate every value they stand for. Conforming to the world at the expense of living for CHRIST can be tragic; reject it!

Conforming to the world at the expense of living for CHRIST can be tragic; reject it!

The world's mold includes modes of thinking, acting, and standards of morality, which all border on the state of mind of the Christian. The Bible's call is for Christians to engage in renewing their minds so they could seek GOD correctly and properly – exclusively, vigorously and consistently. We are not in the world to please people; the irony is that the world is at war with Christianity. Anywhere you find yourself, irrespective of the people there, you must seek the honor of the ONE WHO has called you to HIS glory. That is your main assignment on earth.

Steps in Growing in Intimacy with GOD:

- Be born again

- Read the Bible as a love letter written to you by GOD

- Get the revelation about the Love of GOD

- Understand the dimensions of HIS Love

- Accept the Love of GOD

- Appreciate HIS love

- Decide personalized ways of appreciating GOD's love

- Understand the true nature and character of GOD

- Know that HE has forgiven all your sins – past, present and future

- Praise the LORD always

- Insist on rejoicing always, regardless of what's going on in your life

When you have intimacy with GOD, you will have continual fellowship and praise HIM without asking for anything, because HE has given you all things that pertain to life and godliness. When you are connected with GOD, you will have absolute rest.

CHAPTER 7

DOING EXPLOITS IN THE NAME OF JESUS

Some things particularly encourage Christians to excel in their spiritual lives. One of them is remembering that circumstances, situations and the activities of spirits that are contrary to the word of GOD, can be changed. When these issues arise with seemingly unbearable pressure, some Christians forget who they are and what they carry. Most of the pressure comes when Christians are always thinking about the adverse circumstances as being unchangeable; so, they despair and worry, just like their unbelieving neighbors.

GOD quickened us together with CHRIST, raised us up together with HIM and caused us to sit together with HIM at GOD's right hand in the heavenly places. Therefore, Christians are placed far above all principalities, powers, might, dominion and every name that is named, not only in this world, but also in the world to come. In other words, GOD gave us authority over every authority and power of the devil (Luke 19:10).

This spiritual relocation is significantly necessary for this singular purpose, because in the spirit realm, the devil and his demons witnessed, and fully understand the hierarchical ascendency of the born again child of GOD. Although this does not deter him from attacking the believer, he can do so only in the physical realm – a condition that offers Christians a tremendous advantage to always defeat satan, and maintain CHRIST's victory.

Paul says in Ephesians 6:12, *"For we wrestle not against flesh and blood, but against principalities, and against powers...."*

We have seen previously that the choice of the word "wrestle" depicts a present and on-going contest between believers and the devil, where the struggle to maintain the victory JESUS won for us, is continuous, as long as we are in this present evil world. The great news is that the fight is fixed, with victory on our side!

Verse 11 of the same chapter reveals that the devil's weapon of warfare is deception. Deception could be simple and easy to overcome, but in actual fact, very difficult to realize, primarily because the deceived never knows that he is hooked. As new comers into the kingdom of GOD, like sojourners, we are bound to wander aimlessly if we neglect our roadmap – the scriptural guidelines.

The best advice you can give to Christians who care to listen, is that they should stick to the SCRIPT and they will not miss it! The script here is the scripture. I believe that this is why GOD took on the responsibility of directing our paths (Jeremiah 10:23). Doing the SCRIPT (SCRIPTURE) may not be convenient sometimes and may not even make sense at other times; but according to Ephesians 6: 13-20, it is a GOD-proven buffer against the wiles of the devil.

The last words of David (a man after GOD's own heart) to his son, Solomon, can shed some light on the best strategies in being effective in exercising our GOD-given spiritual authority:

1 Chronicles 28:9 (KJV)

"And thou, Solomon my son, know thou the God of thy father and serve him with a perfect heart and serve HIM with a willing mind: for the LORD searcheth all hearts, and understandeth all the imaginations of the thoughts: if thou seek him, he will be found of thee; but if thou forsake him, he will cast thee off forever."

In everything you do, GOD and godliness should be your priorities. These were David's preoccupation, right from his youth. For example, he never planned to fight Goliath but because the latter dared to challenge GOD, David was instantly ready to take a stand and fight for what he believed. It was obvious that worshipping and honoring GOD were a part of his lifestyle. He did not just practice godliness; he was godly. The book of Psalms has a total of 150 chapters and over 70 of them were credited to David. His relationship with GOD was the totality of who he was. This was also revealed in an important aspect of his life – exercising spiritual authority against satan and his cohorts.

Resist the Devil and he will Flee

James 4:7 (NLT)

"So humble yourselves before God. Resist the devil, and he will flee from you."

There are two outcomes from this verse; when you submit to GOD, you resist the devil and he would flee from you. The devil doesn't have a dominant power to throw things at you, he looks for a way to get into you and use those things against you.

Spiritual authority can be exercised directly by casting out foul spirits and commanding them to leave; affirming the blessings of GOD by speaking the word of GOD in place of the devil's suggestions and activities; and by laying hands on the sick to heal them. For example, when you notice the first sign of pain or ill health in any part of your body, you should speak and command it to leave immediately. That is a more direct exercise of your authority. Healing the sick in the name of JESUS by laying your hand on them is another direct application of your authority.

By the same token, spiritual authority can also be exercised indirectly. This is by ignoring the devil's suggestions and negative activities or resisting the temptation to yield to the suggestions, and go contrary to GOD's word. This may require speaking out loud to yourself the word of GOD which you would rather obey, than the suggestions of the enemy.

An example of a situation where this approach is most useful is in the case of combating depressive moods like discouragement, self-pity, and feelings of condemnation. The first thing to realize is that none of these moods are of GOD. If the precursor of your negative emotion is a sin, then thank GOD for forgiving you your past, present and future sins, and cleansing you from all unrighteousness (1 John 1:9; Hebrews 10:10, 12 & 14). Taking time to thank GOD from the bottom of your heart would restore your peace instantly. So, always make deliberate efforts to maintain the peace and joy of the LORD in your heart; this should always be a priority, or an antidote, against all forms of discouragement (Proverbs 17:22). If your toxic mood is not caused by guilt, but offense or disappointment, remember the same satan that caused the discouraging situation is the same that suggests the negative thoughts that got you depressed. You must recognize it for what it is, rise up, and choose to think and speak GOD's words concerning you, for those situations. Resolve to always thank GOD for all things – the good, the bad and the seemingly ugly, because it is GOD's will for you (1 Thessalonians 5:18).

One of the uniqueness of Christianity is that it is verifiable and evidential, and the word of GOD is law. GOD's word happens when the conditions are met; it is universal, consistent, and impartial. The word "law" is used in different ways in the scriptures and in order to get the different shades of meaning, going as far back as the *1828 Webster Dictionary*, seemed reasonable.

The New Testament expressions (or sense, of the usage of the word) are listed below in the *1828 Webster Dictionary*, which defines a law as:

1. A rule, particularly an established or permanent rule, prescribed by the supreme power of a state to its subjects, for regulating their actions, particularly their social actions.

2. The word of God; the doctrines and precepts of God, or his revealed will. *"But his delight is in the law of the Lord, and in his law doth he meditate day and night." Psalm 1.*

3. A rule or axiom of science or art; settled principle; as the laws of versification or poetry.

4. In general, law is a rule of action prescribed for the government of rational beings or moral agents, to which rule they are bound to yield obedience, in

default of which they are exposed to punishment; or law is a settled mode or course of action or operation in irrational beings and in inanimate bodies.

An ordinary Google Search definition says that a law is a "the system of rules which a particular country or community recognizes as regulating the actions of its members and which it may enforce by the imposition of penalties."

Whether in the Old Testament times, New Testament times, or now, as defined by Google, one common fact about a law is that it is usually enacted to be universally, consistently, and impartially obeyed, and it is applicable to all its subjects. The physical and moral laws follow the same rule: that similar outcomes are expected whenever the conditions of the law are met. The words of the physical and the moral law-giver (GOD) are laws in themselves.

If the Word says for example, *"A merry heart does good [like] a medicine: but a broken spirit dries the bones"* (Proverbs 17:22, NKJV), then whosoever makes an effort to maintain a joyful heart would experience good health. It is the law. It is an effective way to resist the devil of discouragement and depressive moods. Praise the LORD!

How Do You Avoid Being Deceived?

Ephesians 6:11 reveals that the devil comes against us with deception; so, resisting satan's wiles means resisting his deceptions. The question then would be: how do you know that you are not being deceived? Unfortunately, deception is notorious for being difficult to detect at face value, because mendacious deceivers package their lies in the most palatable and appealing ways, such that the most brilliant or the "elects of GOD" can be deceived.

It is common knowledge that deception is not a function of age, educational attainment, social status, gender, race, marital status or profession. Even a deceiver can, himself, be deceived. Deception is one of the many concepts that a Christian should not fall prey to, because GOD made provision for us not to be deceived.

Christians make many decisions and choices on a daily basis. Often we, like the unbelievers, don't know, at face value, which way to go, especially when we try to go without GOD. However, if we trust that the LORD knows better, and although HE gave us the free will, it is HIS responsibility to direct our paths (Jeremiah 10:23), then we should acknowledge HIM in ALL our ways, and NOT lean on our own understanding (Proverbs 3:5-6).

There are many things you can do to avoid being deceived, but sticking to the script is the most reliable antidote against deception. This applies to whether or not we are making decisions or choosing from alternative options as well as deciding on the right response to a bad situation. In the book of Acts, Chapter 16, when Paul and Silas got thrown into prison for preaching the gospel, rather than holding a pity-party, crying, or even praying, they chose to praise the LORD.

Binding and casting out demons could have been a nice thing to do but Paul and Silas chose to sing praises unto GOD. The scripture says to give GOD thanks in ALL things (1Thessalonians 5:18), so give GOD thanks! Pray about everything, don't worry about anything, and give GOD thanks for all things (Philippians 4:6 NLT). I know some of you have thanked GOD for your bad and ugly situations before, but I wish that you would remember to do it always. Same goes for me too!

When my phone broke in the first week of February, 2020, I took the time to thank the LORD for my phone. Later, when my son found out that I did not get a new or functional phone, he wondered, out loud, why I was thanking the LORD for my phone. I told him that I was thanking GOD for my broken phone. Even though we can hypothesize why GOD wants us to thank HIM for everything, I do recognize that HE, GOD, is wiser than I could ever be; thus, sticking to the script by thanking HIM, was the wisest thing to do at that moment. By thanking GOD, I avoided being sad, or depressed about the prospect of not having a phone for a couple of days. There may be some other spiritual value for thanking GOD for all things, but for me, simply obeying HIS word was the necessary and sufficient reason to do it!

In 1991, I was transferred to Queens College, Yaba, Nigeria and I stayed with one of my colleagues in her parents' house in Festac Town, Lagos, because my husband was staying with his cousin and they could only accommodate one of us at the time. One Friday evening at about 7 p.m., my colleague asked me to leave their home first thing the next morning. All attempts to find out why, failed. I was asking mainly, so I could apologize but she refused to tell me why. The number of weeks we agreed for me to stay was not yet up, but I was told to leave. The ejection posed a couple of problems. It was too late to go tell my husband and I couldn't call him because we did not have cell phones at that time in Nigeria. In preparation for an early morning trip, I got my belongings ready to leave the next morning. Meanwhile, I started praising the LORD! I genuinely prayed and thanked the LORD for the situation, till the very early hours of the morning. Then I fell into a trance where the LORD set me on a mountain top from where I gave light to a multitude of people. Instead of trying to figure out for myself what may have gone wrong, I chose to spend the rest of the evening gratefully praising the LORD! In the process of thanking and praising GOD, I was given the first part of the vision of the purpose of GOD for my life! In the midst of what should have been a pity-party, GOD called me to be a light bearer for HIS people. What an honor! My joy new no bounds, as I gladly received the call. Praise the LORD!

In the two examples given above, I chose to praise the

LORD, instead of wallowing either in self-pity or anger. Because I chose to thank and praise the LORD, I was neither depressed nor discouraged (which is the devil's Number One target).

The truth is that you have a choice: you can get upset or disappointed when circumstances, situations, or the devil strikes with his wiles, but if you turn the moment to a time of praise and worship unto the LORD as soon as possible, satan would have failed in his plans against you. You may say that some of these may be "easier said than done", and this is understandable, but with deliberate practice, it does become easier.

The joy of the LORD is your strength (Nehemiah 8:10) against all the wiles of the devil. Refusing to allow the devil any parking-space in your heart, is an effective way of resisting satan. I have often thought of offense as a double jeopardy: satan orchestrates an incident to offend and generate sadness. Then, the same satan tempts you, causing you not to thank GOD for the situation – a catalyst for depression!

> *Deuteronomy 28:47-48 (NKJV)*
>
> *47 "Because you did not serve the LORD your God with joy and gladness of heart, for the abundance of everything,*
>
> *48 therefore you shall serve your enemies, whom the LORD will send against you, in hun-*

*ger, in thirst, in nakedness, and in need of ev-
erything; and He will put a yoke of iron on your
neck until He has destroyed you."*

When you don't worship and thank the LORD for everything, the chances are increased for you to be sad and
depressed. Unhappiness and happiness share the same
unique place in your heart; therefore, they are mutually exclusive, meaning that you cannot be genuinely happy and
sad at the exact, same time. When you allow yourself to
feel offense deep in your heart, you cannot find joy there
at the same time. So, to restore your joy, you must get rid
of the enemy that is occupying your heart, by choosing to
thank and praise GOD for that situation, regardless of how
bad the incident or situation was.

Thank GOD long and deep, to the point that you feel
the gratitude in your heart, and until the sadness has been
displaced with joy. Be deliberate in pulling down all the
negative thoughts that are contrary to the word of GOD (2
Corinthians 10:4-5) by speaking out audibly to your hearing (Romans 10:10). Then, speak and affirm what the Bible
says concerning you that are direct opposites of the negative thoughts. Also, as much as possible, pray for the individual who offended you. This would reduce the chances of
harboring ill feelings against him.

Each of the circumstances and events that bring offense, provides opportunity for satan to get an upper hand

over your emotions, by attacking your strength and faith through taking your joy. If you faint in the day of adversity, then your strength is small or under attack. (Proverbs 24:10). Here lies the centerpiece of the word of GOD: thanking HIM for the offense, which leads to forgiveness.

If you don't forgive, satan has deceived you into opening the door for your faith or strength to be attacked.

Proverbs 24:10 (NKJV)

"If you faint in the day of adversity, your strength is small [mine-under attack]."

Proverbs 24:10 reveals that what causes Christians to faint under the weight of adversity, is not the adversity itself, but the quality of their strength. When you study the meaning of "strength" in this verse it is synonymous with faith. It is like a supply pipe to your resolve to beat the odds in your life. Your strength being small, means that the supply chain to your faith, to enable you to resist satan is under attack; it is weakened, or inactive. When that happens, deception is closer to you than ever.

Daniel 11 reveals something about using GOD'S grace to avoid being deceived. (Read the entire chapter to get more insight into the context). It is about a vision GOD gave to Daniel concerning an impending outcome of the Jews disobeying and ignoring the word of GOD. Many Bible scholars believe that the prophecy has occurred. The prophecy specifically stated that those who broke their covenant with the LORD of Heaven will be deceived and be carried away captives. However, those who know their GOD, those who have intimate relationship with GOD, shall not be moved; they would be strong and do great exploits.

Daniel 11:32 (KJV)

"And such as do wickedly against the covenant shall he corrupt by flatteries: but the people that do know their God shall be strong, and do exploits."

For intimacy with GOD to involve the totality of who you are, it must reflect in what you accept and love and what you don't. For example, if Kanye West is a celebrity because he is a great rapper for the world, he cannot be your own celebrity, if he is against CHRIST and the people of GOD. However, Kanye West is my celebrity because I know he loves JESUS and is not ashamed to identify with the people of GOD. As Christians, our criteria for determining celebrities are different and should be for you, if you desire intimacy with CHRIST.

For example, while researching the positions of some presidential candidates some time ago, I came across a speech made by one of them (the then Candidate Barak Obama) where he was making a mockery of JESUS's Sermon on the Mount. Instantly, I crossed that candidate off my list. On the other hand, all GOD's Generals that I know, both alive and dead, are my celebrities. My current and former Pastors and their associate pastors, are my celebrities. My brothers and sisters in the church, including those who do very little, are my celebrities, and I honor them (1 Corinthians 12:23).

How Do You Develop and Grow?

1. A heart of extreme gratitude

Psalm 30:4 (NKJV)

"Sing praise to the LORD, you saints of His, and give thanks at the remembrance of His holy name."

David said to sing praise to the LORD and thank HIM as often as you remember HIM, which should be all the time.

Psalm 9:1 (NKJV): (A Psalm of David).

"I will praise [You,] O LORD, with my whole heart; I will tell of all Your marvelous works."

Praise at all times and focus on HIS great work and love for you. Your salvation is the chief of HIS great works!

2. Content and comprehensiveness

GOD and CHRIST must be the object of your adoration and love for HIS people.

Matthew 22:37-39 (NKJV)

37 "Jesus said to him, 'You shall love the LORD your God with all your heart, with all your soul, and with all your mind.'

38 This is [the] first and great commandment.

39 And [the] second [is] like it: 'You shall love your neighbor as yourself.'"

The content of all you do, regardless where and with whom, needs to be centered on GOD (Colossians 3:23-24). When the Bible says to do all things heartily unto the LORD, it really means everything.

3. Intentionality and resoluteness

No one becomes intimate with GOD by accident; it must be deliberate and engaging.

Jeremiah 29:13 (NKJV)

"And you will seek Me and find [Me,] when you search for Me with all your heart."

W.A. Tozah taught that the act of being born again should be an act of the total personality, where the intellect, mind, will, conscience and emotions of an individual are engaged in the belief of JESUS. Titus 1:16 condemned people who claimed the love GOD but denied HIS existence by their lifestyle.

JESUS also talked about people who could cast out

devils in HIS name, but were never known in the kingdom. Thus, evidence abounds that one needs to be intentional and resolute about his relationship with GOD in order to develop and increase in his intimacy with HIM. Be resolute and intentional in your pursuit of GOD.

4. Constancy and consistency

The world is always changing but GOD does not change and HIS obligations towards HIS children do not change. The scripture, in Hebrews 13:8 (NKJV) says that JESUS CHRIST is the same yesterday, today, and forever. GOD is everyone's contemporary. HE does not grow old, tired or uninterested. HE is omniscient; therefore, HE is not surprised by the development and advancements of man and the universe HE made. So, why should change in culture and ideologies change your views about GOD and HIS word? The world could change and provide technological advancements that enhance your access to and the study of GOD's word, but it must not change your views and sound biblical response to GOD and HIS word. Be consistent in following CHRIST like Peter in John 6:68, who insisted on following CHRIST because HE has "words that give live"(NLT).

Hebrews 13:5 (NKJV)

"Let your conduct be without covetousness; be content with such things as you have. For He Himself has said, 'I will never leave you nor forsake you.'"

John 6:68 (NLT) Simon Peter replied, "Lord, to whom would we go? You have the words that give eternal life.

5. Promptness and Decisiveness

1 Kings 18:21 (NKJV)

"And Elijah came to all the people, and said, 'How long will you falter between two opinions? If the LORD is God, follow Him; but if Baal, follow him.' But the people answered him not a word."

Be ready and quick to respond to HIS promptings. For instance, David was prompt and decisive in dealing with Goliath.

To develop a reputation in the spiritual realm as GOD'S General, who wins every battle, you must be alert to cut all ties and respond promptly as the situation requires. Satan does not play fair, so take authority immediately, as soon as you recognize the attack. When GOD gives you an instruction that requires immediate attention, do not hesitate or consult many people before you respond. Be quick on your feet to respond and take steps to stop satan before he gains a strong foothold. Paul is an example of someone who did not confer with anyone to prepare and take on the assignment GOD gave him (Galatians 1:16). Being decisive is an important part of exercising your spiritual authority.

Although James was talking about seeking GOD's wisdom, but he highlighted an essential connection between decisiveness and faith (James 1:5-7). According to The Passion Translation:

Just make sure you are empowered by confident faith without doubting

James 1:5-7

5 "if anyone longs to be wise, ask God for wisdom and he will give it! He won't see your lack of wisdom as an opportunity to scold you over your failures but he will overwhelm your failures with his generous grace.[d]

6 **Just make sure you are empowered by confident faith without doubting** *that you will receive. For the ambivalent person believes one minute and doubts the next.* **Being undecided** *makes you become like the rough seas driven and tossed by the wind. You're up one minute and tossed down the next.*

7–8 When you are half-hearted and wavering it leaves you unstable.[e] Can you really expect to receive anything from the Lord when you're in that condition?

The above passage calls for a resolution to promptly respond to and approach GOD with confidence that HE is trustworthy!.

In summary:

The only antidote to deception is knowing the truth

and insisting on the truth even if it kills you!

Doing the SCRIPT (SCRIPTURE) may not be convenient sometimes, and may not even make sense at other times; however, it is a GOD-proven buffer against the wiles of the devil, according to Ephesians 6: 13-20 and 2 Corinthians 10:4-5.

CHAPTER 8

SPIRITUAL OVERRIDE

Matthew 28:19-20 (NKJV)

19 "Go therefore and make disciples of all the nations, baptizing them in the name of the Father and of the Son and of the Holy Spirit,

20 teaching them to observe all things that I have commanded you; and lo, I am with you always, even to the end of the age. Amen."

JESUS specifically instructed the HIS disciples to teach their converts to "observe all things" that HE had taught them. With regards to the authority HE gave them, let's review some of the "things" JESUS wanted new converts to learn (John 17: 18-20). The pattern is that, as JESUS sent HIS disciples to teach others, then the converted "others" would go on and teach a new set of "others" to observe all things that JESUS had taught HIS disciples.

After selecting the twelve apostles (Matthew 10:2-4), JESUS sent them (Matthew 10:5) with power and authority to cast out unclean spirits, and to "heal all kinds of sickness and all kinds of disease."

As can be seen in Matthew 10:1, JESUS gave them supernatural authority and power to enforce obedience on unclean spirits, sicknesses and diseases. They transcended the natural realm and worked in the spiritual realm.

> *Matthew 10:1 (NKJV)*
>
> *"And when He had called His twelve disciples to [Him,] He gave them power over unclean spirits, to cast them out, and to heal all kinds of sickness and all kinds of disease."*
>
> *Matthew 10:7-8 (NKJV)*
>
> *7 "And as you go, preach, saying, 'The kingdom of heaven is at hand.'*
>
> *8 Heal the sick, cleanse the lepers, and raise the dead, cast out demons. Freely you have received, freely give."*

An important aspect of the instructions, was to exercise their authority as freely as they had received it. Luke's account of the same scripture in Matthew 10:1 reads thus:

> *Luke 9:1 (NKJV)*
>
> *"Then He called His twelve disciples together and gave them **power and authority over all demons, and to cure diseases.**"*

Observe that JESUS gave HIS disciples power, and HE gave them authority over ALL demons and to cure the diseases. Thus, you and I have power and authority over all demons! Later, JESUS sent a set of seventy disciples to preach the gospel (Luke 10:1) and to heal the sick (Luke 10:9). The seventy returned rejoicing that demons had obeyed them in the name of JESUS.

Luke 10:17 (NKJV)

"Then the seventy returned with joy, saying, 'Lord, even the demons are subject to us in your name.'"

JESUS reminded them that satan had fallen and that they had authority and power over all the powers of satan. HE also reminded them that entering into heaven was more important than possessing the ability to cast out devils (Verse 20).

Luke 10:19 (NKJV)

*"Behold, I give you the authority to trample on serpents and scorpions, and **over all the power of the enemy,** and **nothing shall by any means hurt you.**"*

In HIS teaching, JESUS told HIS disciples in Luke 10:19, that their victory and safety were guaranteed, as "nothing shall by any means hurt" them.

We also see three things:

Therefore, we have a GOD-given authority to override all the authority and power of the devil in all his forms and manifestations! Praise JESUS!

1. We have authority over ALL the abilities and possibilities of satan.

2. We have ability and power that accompany our authority.

3. Our safety is guaranteed!

Therefore, we have a GOD-given authority to override all the authority and power of the devil in all his forms and manifestations! Praise JESUS!

JESUS, in Mark 16:15-20, was more explicit in extending to HIS disciples' proselytes, the authority and power to cast out devils and to heal the sick.

Mark 16:15-18 (NKJV)

15 "And He said to them, 'Go into all the world and preach the gospel to every creature.

16 He who believes and is baptized will be saved; but he who does not believe will be condemned.

17 And these signs will follow those who believe: In My name they will cast out demons; they will speak with new tongues;

18 they will take up serpents; and if they drink anything deadly, it will by no means hurt them; they will lay hands on the sick, and they will recover.'"

Spiritual Override

A number of points can be made from Mark 16:15-18. It is evident that these rights and privileges accompanied the "believing" ones. They are not add-on gifts, like the gifts of the Spirit listed in Ephesians 4, Roman 12, 1 Corinthians 12, and 14. They were an integral part of the believer's make-up at his spiritual birth. The baptism of the HOLY GHOST definitely ensures that you have power on you, which accentuates the boldness to exercise the authority. Being born again means GOD giving birth to a brand new spirit in you. This tells everyone who believes in JESUS CHRIST that HE is the Son of GOD and the "propitiation" for all sins (1 John 2:2).

Once you are born again, you are now a son. GOD unites your brand new born-again spirit with the spirit of HIS SON, JESUS CHRIST. You actually have in you, from that point, the power of GOD that raised JESUS CHRIST from the dead. All this authority and power is important for engaging in the heavy spiritual warfare against the power of evil in and around you. However, this book focuses on seeing the value of living life from your born-again spirit, rather than leaning on the wisdom of your flesh. The Bible says that the flesh profits nothing. Your flesh profits nothing (John 6:63), especially in responding to spiritually motivated situations.

The authority and power given to believers is an essential part of the "things" the disciples were to teach their converts. Although some of the instructions were addressed to JESUS's disciples directly, everything they learned was for them as well as us, whom they would teach. You should have confidence in the words of JESUS that although not specifically addressing you, that power would work for you in as great a measure as it worked for JESUS, and even in a greater measure (John 14:12), if you believe.

We saw earlier that we are assured victory each time we resist satan, and that he would flee from us (James 4:7, NKJV), as long as we are submitted to GOD.

According to Ephesians 6:10-11, with the complete armory of spiritual weapons we can successfully resist the wiles of the enemy. *The Phillips Translation* says, *"Put on God's complete armor so that you can successfully resist all the devil's methods of attack."*

Some people believe that satan does not have any abilities at all, but uses the power of deception to hurt the children of GOD; and some believe the devil does possess some power with which he attacks Christians. *The Phillips Translation* ends the argument, and indicates that you have access to all the authority, power, and every divine instrumentation to resist, trample upon, cast down strong holds, and utterly destroy all the activities, plans and purposes of the enemy, against you and your loved ones.

Ephesians 6:12 makes it clear that all our conflicts,

difficulties, lack, sicknesses and diseases, and all forms of challenges (contrary to what GOD has given us) come from satan. 2 Corinthians 10:3-5 and Ephesians 6:13-18 tell us to engage with GOD's armory and HIS word, to fend off satan's attacks, knowing who we are, acknowledging what we have (all CHRIST's authority and power), and taking a stand with GOD, in exercising our authority.

Ephesians 6:10-18 (The Philips Translation)

"In conclusion be strong - not in yourselves but in the Lord, in the power of his boundless resource. Put on God's complete armour so that you can successfully resist all the devil's methods of attack. For our fight is not against any physical enemy: it is against organisations and powers that are spiritual. We are up against the unseen power that controls this dark world, and spiritual agents from the very headquarters of evil. Therefore you must wear the whole armour of God that you may be able to resist evil in its day of power, and that even when you have fought to a standstill you may still stand your ground. Take your stand then with truth as your belt, righteousness your breastplate, the Gospel of peace firmly on your feet, salvation as your helmet and in your hand the sword of the Spirit, the Word of God. Above all be sure you take faith as your shield, for it can quench every burning missile the enemy hurls at you. Pray at all times with every kind of spiritual prayer, keeping alert and persistent as you pray for all Christ's men and women."

So, JESUS admonishes that we should have faith in GOD and GOD only (Mark 11:22). Where mountains in our lives represent difficulties, challenges and obstacles, we have whatever it takes to change and move things forward, in alignment with the word of GOD for us.

The gospel truth is that you have authority and power that must trump the wiles and power of the enemy. As of the day of this teaching, there was no known definition of "spiritual authority" found on any of the popular search engines like Google and Yahoo, and any dictionary. I believe that the reason is because spiritual authority pertains to the Spirit of GOD and can only be spiritually discerned (1 Corinthians 2:14).

> *1 Corinthians 2:13-15 (NKJV)*
>
> *13 "These things we also speak, not in words which man's wisdom teaches but which the Holy Spirit teaches, comparing spiritual things with spiritual.*
>
> *14 But the natural man does not receive the things of the Spirit of God, for they are foolishness to him; nor can he know [them,] because they are spiritually discerned.*
>
> *15 But he who is spiritual judges all things, yet he himself is [rightly] judged by no one."*

As soon as you believe and are born again, you have the authority to parade yourself as a son of GOD and because you are a son, you belong to CHRIST, and you are an heir of GOD and a joint heir with JESUS CHRIST – an heir according to the promise GOD made to Abraham (Galatians 3:29). Because you are a son, the Spirit of CHRIST lives in you, and the power in you is equivalent to the power that raised CHRIST from the dead. Therefore, you have access to and can discern spiritual things, so that you can act appropriately to demolish all opposing forces of darkness. Praise the LORD!

Spirit Life Trumps Living from the Flesh

If you believe in your heart and confess with your mouth that JESUS is the SON of GOD, then you receive HIM as your LORD and SAVIOR, you become a son (John 1:12-13; Romans 10:8-10, 13). As a son, you have authority, power, and all the armory of GOD's weaponry against the enemy, but that would not insulate you from satanic attacks. GOD, in HIS love, gave us specific instructions throughout the Bible on how to be effective in resisting satan and his wiles. For example, we are instructed to present our bodies as living sacrifices to GOD (Romans 12:1) and renew our minds so that we do not live in the world view of unbelievers (Romans 12:2).

The wiles, deceptions and most of the ways the devil attacks a believer are through the mind, but we have authority to tear down all the lies of the devil. The recommended weapons of warfare, for believers, are spiritual. Fighting from a spiritual vantage point, rather than the physical, ensures your chances of winning. Satan is the master of the flesh – the father of lies, manipulations (Ephesians 6:11), lust of the eyes, lust of the flesh, and pride of life (1 John 2:16). You can't beat the devil at his game.

You are much more powerful in the spirit, because the weapons of your warfare are spiritual, not physical; but you are a novice, compared to satan, when it comes to physical weaponry. You can, however, excel in utilizing physical weapons if they are positioned as an extension of and the demonstration of your spiritual authority. I will explain this further in the next section.

Let me explain with an example: a physical weapon will be effective in combating adversarial attack from an individual after you have bound satan's influence behind the scenes; then, physically you can settle the matter with either stern, but kind words (Ephesians 4:15), or pleasant words (Proverbs 16:24), depending on the context. The secret, always, is to remember that although we are in the flesh, we do not win with carnal (physical) weapons.

2 Corinthians 10:3-5 (NKJV)

3 "For though we walk in the flesh, we do not

war according to the flesh.

4 For the weapons of our warfare [are] not carnal but mighty in God for pulling down strongholds,

5 casting down arguments and every high thing that exalts itself against the knowledge of God, bringing every thought into captivity to the obedience of Christ."

I will take an example from a story by Kenneth Hagin. In 1942, while he was pastoring in East Texas, he had a situation bothering him in his body and didn't tell anyone about it, except the LORD. He prayed and believed the LORD would heal him. Then, he had a dream that he was walking and talking with another minister in some kind of parade ground or ball field.

All of a sudden, the minister with him jumped and exclaimed, "Look!"

He turned around and saw two ferocious, roaring lions. They both took to their heels, but Brother Hagin realized that they would never make it to safety in good time. He stopped dead still and went back to meet the lions that were moving towards him with fangs bared and roaring.

He spoke out loud: "I resist you in the name of JESUS! You can't hurt me." Immediately, they ran up to him like a couple of kittens, sniffed around his ankles and paid no attention to him.

When he woke up, he knew that the physical battle he had been fighting was already won, and instantly the symptoms disappeared. He had stood his ground and wouldn't give in, and he won.

I came home one Sunday after service with a book, *The Believer's Authority* by Kenneth E. Hagin (2001), which I read on my knees. I finished the book in a sitting because I was fascinated by all the power and authority GOD gives to believers to override satan's activities. With a heart filled with awe for and gratitude to GOD, I spent most of the rest of the day praising the LORD. In my dream that night, I saw all kinds of imaginable animals, wild, carnivorous, mild, and friendly beasts of the earth lined up on opposite sides of my driveway facing each other. As I stepped out of my house to walk down my driveway, all the animals bowed in unison, indicating their obeisance and loyalty to me. When I woke up, I realized that GOD showed me in that one instance the dominion HE has given us in CHRIST JESUS!

Being a son of GOD is a privilege given by GOD to believers (because of JESUS) to enforce obedience on any and everything that concerns us, which is not aligned with what GOD has said concerning us. In the words of A.W. Tozar, "Being born again must be an aggressive act of the total personality and not a passive acceptance" of JESUS

CHRIST as our LORD and SAVIOR. (See my book on *What It Really Means To Be Born Again*).

To be born again literally means that GOD, who is a Spirit (John 4:24), gives birth to a brand-new spirit in you. HE did not pick up your old spirit, dust it up, clean it, or revive it, no; HE created you anew in righteousness and true holiness (Ephesians 4:24) with power and authority to act on HIS behalf as needed.

Proverbs 20:27 (NKJV)

"The spirit of a man is the lamp of the LORD, searching all the inner depths of his heart."

The spirit that lived in you before your new birth was dead (Genesis 2:16-17) because of Adam's sin. It was corrupt and incapable of living right. Since the spirit of a man is the candle of the LORD (Proverbs 20:27) and GOD's eyes cannot look upon wickedness (Habakkuk 1:13) the spirit of man needed to be righteous and holy.

However, man could not earn righteousness and holiness on his own, because even if he could keep all the laws of GOD, (which he couldn't), the conditions or motives of his heart were equally important in producing righteousness (1 Corinthians 13:1-3). Since the law could not produce righteousness (Galatians 3:21b), GOD's pre-designed plan of salvation (1 Peter 1:19-20; 2 Timothy 1:9; Titus 1:2) that consists of eternal life and the gift of righteousness and holiness in the newly-created spirit at the new birth (2 Corinthians 5:21; Ephesians 4:24), came into being.

Whereas GOD can and does communicate and fellowship with a believer in the spiritual realm, yet, for all the benefits and gifts of GOD to manifest in the physical, his mind needs to be in agreement with his newly created spirit. GOD makes available everything in the spirit format, but the natural man cannot receive the things of the Spirit of GOD, because they are spiritually discerned (2 Corinthians 2:13-14). This is one reason being born again is very important. Being born again is not just about being fair or being a good person, telling the truth, and so on; it is about being made suitable for the indwelling Spirit of CHRIST by receiving the only reconciliation with GOD available to man.

I am sure we can find some people with better character and integrity than some Christians, but being born again is not a character modification. The problem was that GOD, WHO is a Spirit, needed to dwell in man to cause man to "follow my decrees and be careful to obey my regulations" (Ezekiel 36:27; NLT). Thus, HE created a brand new spirit in man with a seed of righteousness and holiness (2 Corinthians 5:21).

The seed of righteousness is what propels you towards doing right. This is opposed to the life you lived as a sinner, when you were irresistibly attracted towards evil because of the seed of sin or the sin nature in you. On the other hand, as a son of GOD, righteousness is one of the gifts you are endowed with. It is a gift, given to Christians by the Spirit of GOD, and it is part and parcel of the right of every born-again Christian. This is unlike the gift of working of miracles and discerning of spirits, which is only given to some.

Every born-again Christian is loaded with blessings in the heavenly places (Ephesians 1:3), all good things that pertain to life and godliness (2 Peter 1:3), and is highly favored (Ephesians 1:6). Little wonder that John exclaimed at the magnanimity of the FATHER's love in making us HIS sons (1 John 3:1). Taking time to meditate on GOD's love for you is transformative and makes you want to do all things heartily unto HIM, as an expression of your gratitude. Then, you will consistently find yourself deliberately living righteously (because that's your new default mode) than you lived in the past. The reason you have the power of GOD in you is because you are one with HIS SON, and all the power is HIS (Matthew 28:18-20) and HE is one with you (1 Corinthians 6:17). Praise the LORD!

Moreover, maintaining your new default mode of righteous living, requires renewing your mind (Romans 12:2). Renewing the mind means to dethrone and replace every carnal strategy and world view, with GOD's word. As sons of GOD, we belong in HIS kingdom (John 17:16). We are in the world but we are not of the world. Our kingdom is spiritual and GOD did not leave us the option of living life from the flesh.

This fundamental of spiritual authority is not necessarily about casting out devils, but more about knowing how powerful you are in the spirit and how you can effectively take advantage of it. This fundamental of spiritual authority is not necessarily about casting out devils, but more about knowing how powerful you are in the spirit and how you can effectively take advantage of it. The Bible is very explicit about what works effectively in engaging the spirit realm.

The Spirit Gives Life

John 6:63 (NKJV)

"It is the Spirit who gives life; the flesh profits nothing. The words that I speak to you are spirit, and [they] are life."

1 Timothy 4:8 says that physical exercise profit only a little, but John 6:63 tells us that the flesh profits nothing. This means that there is no advantage or profit in it. As sons of GOD, to be effective on this earth, the Bible is saying that living from the flesh has no benefit, but living on the word of GOD is life-giving and peaceful because it is the spirit that can reach and affect everything.

Romans 8:6 (NKJV)

"For to be carnally minded is death, but to be spiritually minded is life and peace."

"To be carnally minded" is the same as saying that you are living from your flesh, and Paul says that it is equivalent to death. Comparing the word "death" in Romans 8:6 to "death" in other passages in the Bible, we know that it means that the individual would suffer lack, debt, weakness, challenges, problems, sicknesses, diseases and all kinds of the oppressions of the devil, until the individual finally dies physically, then end up in hell fire.

In Genesis 2:16-17, GOD told Adam and Eve that they would die if they ate the fruit of the tree of good and evil. They disobeyed GOD and ate the forbidden fruit. Although, they did not drop dead instantly, something happened to their spiritual well-being which resulted in shame, agony and other ills, until they eventually died physically.

Romans 5:12 says that death came into the world through disobedience, and a careful examination of what followed afterwards shows that suffering of all kinds came into the world through Adam's disobedience. Drawing insight from Genesis 2, we can conclude that to be carnally minded is equivalent to introducing suffering and every kind of mishap that leads, not only to physical death, but to the permanent separation from the benefits of the death and resurrection of JESUS (at least in this world). Romans 8:6 is saying that if your default mode is acting from the flesh, although it might not end up in a physical death instantly, the outcome or end result will amount to nothing.

To be spiritually minded, on the other hand, is life giving, rejuvenating, creative, innovative, and gives peace of mind, regardless of what is going on. GOD laid bare for us everything about how HE wants us to live, and how HE wants us to conduct ourselves in order to be victorious on earth. If you notice, these instructions for victorious Christian living are for our good and our good always. (Deuteronomy 6:24). Obeying them or not does not add or take away from the greatness of GOD, but it does limit the manifestations of HIS plans of greatness and prosperity in all aspects of your life (Psalm 78:41).

I am not trying to minimize some of the things that we face on a daily basis, and how we are constantly inundated by the desires of the flesh everywhere and in everything around us. I understand that in our physical body, we get bombarded with all kinds of negative thoughts and desires continuously. Sometimes, we get so tired and confused that we may be tempted to forget who we are, whose we are and what we carry. That was why, earlier, I gave you a list of how to get yourself engaged in spiritual exercises, to help you outpace the fast-moving world around you. I mentioned the need to be intentional in your approach. If you want to constantly remember and remind yourself of who you are and how to get to where you are headed, you have to be deliberate.

Always engage the HOLY SPIRIT by praying in

tongues, to build yourself up (Jude 1:20). Do not allow anger or any offense occupy your mind beyond the promptings of the Spirit of GOD. As GOD's son, the HOLY SPIRIT is always there to remind you of the word of GOD you already know, to help you think differently at that moment. Be sure to oblige HIM, and the more you yield to HIM, the more you will be open to hear and follow HIS leading in your life. For me, I can say that I have not arrived yet, but I can guarantee you that I am much better today than when I first got the revelations that I am sharing in this book.

Developing and growing in intimacy with CHRIST does not happen by accident. You have to be intentional. As Jeremiah 29:13 says, you shall find GOD, when you search for HIM with all of your heart; not a part, but all of your heart. This means your entire faculties: your soul; your mind, your will, your emotions, your five senses, your strength, your finances, and everything that matters to you. It implies engaging every aspect of your life in spiritual activities so that you can create a memory lane in your mind for the things of GOD that you want to remember. Another aspect of engaging every aspect of your heart has something to do with your choice of the friends and acquaintances that spend time with you regularly, as well as the world's ideologies and views that you identify with. The Bible says that evil communication corruptsq good manners (1 Corinthians 15:33), and instructs explicitly that we come out from them (2 Corinthians 6:17; Revelation 18:4).

GOD, who made human brains and knows that it cannot remember things without making a deliberate effort, instructed the children of Israel on how to remember HIS miracles and the words that HE spoke to them. When GOD wanted the Jews to remember HIS word to them, HE asked them to teach it to their children, write it at their doorposts, on the hem of their garments, and so on. In Deuteronomy 6:1-8, HE asked them to seek HIM diligently and the purpose was so that they would be careful to do HIS word.

Josiah 1:8 has similar instructions about being deliberate in keeping the words before them all the day long so they could remember to do it. HE explained it as the only means to success and prosperity in GOD. GOD knows how our brains work, that our brains would get occupied with whatever is happening in our immediate environment, therefore, HE instructed that we intentionally pursue remembering HIS word.

The advancement in technology, which has multiplied channels for the dissemination of the gospel, has also created more challenges for present-day Christians. Today, we have ample opportunities to be distracted, even during a worship service, but you can become intentional in being engaged during a service. For example, if you deliberately read referenced scriptures and write down your understanding of what the preacher/teacher is saying when a message is going on, they engrave what can be described as a memory lane in your brain, so that later in the privacy of your home, they would help you recall some of the truth you heard.

Similarly, during worship, get engaged with the words of the worship song; let them mean something to you. If the words of the songs don't apply to you, add words that make sense or apply to you and worship your GOD from your heart. When you do, there would be little or no distraction for you during a church service and you would be more likely to remember the words you either heard from the preaching or from the worship sessions, and use as you need them.

Living life from the spirit requires looking at everything, as well as judging and responding to all things spiritually (1 Corinthians 2:14). There is a spiritual meaning or implication for everything physical, since the things we see come from things we don't see (Hebrews 11:3b). Spiritual Christians evaluate all things spiritually to ensure they apply the right spiritual response, understanding that the things we see are temporary (2 Corinthians 4:18) and that we can change them.

2 Corinthians 4:18 (KJV)

While we look not at the things which are seen, but at the things which are not seen: for the things which are seen [are] temporal; but the things which are not seen [are] eternal.

Praying and hearing from GOD are two constants to

spirit-filled believers, but your prayers and what you hear, must not contradict the word of GOD. The most spiritual and accurate way to respond to issues is thinking, speaking and doing the word of GOD (John 6:63).

The Worldly or Fleshly Point of View

The fleshly ways of looking at things can be summarized in the words of 1 Corinthians 1:21-22:

> 21 *"For since, in the wisdom of God, the world through wisdom did not know God, it pleased God through the foolishness of the message preached to save those who believe.*
>
> 22 *For Jews request a sign, and Greeks seek after wisdom."*

We know that the preaching (referenced above) was about preaching the love of GOD as expressed in JESUS's crucifixion and resurrection. There is a great lesson to learn from verse 21. GOD came to man by the way of the cross, because man could not comprehend and embrace GOD and the things about the Spirit of GOD (1 Corinthians 2:14) by their human wisdom. No one could know and become intimate with HIM through logical reasoning and the wisdom of men.

This is so because natural men cannot discern the things about the Spirit of GOD. Of course, those who are not born again, those who do not have a newly created spirit in them, are not capable of receiving things about the Spirit of GOD, because they are beyond their reach (1 Corinthians 2:14). Unbelievers do have access to the spirit world, but not to the spiritual kingdom of GOD. Remember that there are other spirits like satan and his demons, as well as the dead spirit of unbelievers.

Another point raised in Verse 22 is that the natural mind erroneously seeks personal gain, either materially or intellectually, based on the limited perverse wisdom of man. GOD was explicit in Hebrews 11:6 that HE rewards those who diligently seek HIM; therefore, gain is implied in all forms of worship and service to GOD. However, the gains GOD promises are never packaged in the format which carnal minds would want them. GOD is not a slot machine, as in the Casinos. Spiritual things are spiritually discerned!

1 Corinthians 2:14-15 (NKJV)

14 "But the natural man does not receive the things of the Spirit of God, for they are foolishness to him; nor can he know them because they are spiritually discerned.

15 But he who is spiritual judges all things, yet he himself is [rightly] judged by no one."

The reason that spiritual things are foolishness to the natural mind is because GOD dwells in a realm that transcends the five senses of the logical mind. GOD is not sensate, and never plans to be. People who either don't believe or behave as if GOD exists are completely immersed in a "five-sense dimensional world" – a very limited world. They seek to see, taste, smell, hear and feel, such that any experience that fails the five-dimensional test, is disregarded and relegated to the realm of foolishness and offenses.

1 Corinthians 2:15 (NLT)

"Those who are spiritual can evaluate all things, but they themselves cannot be evaluated by others."

Those who are spiritual always seek to evaluate all things spiritually. The Jews seek for signs and the Greek are attracted by the wisdom of men, and therein is the world view about existence and knowledge of GOD: What is in it for me? Does it appeal to my five senses?

When the Jews asked JESUS for a sign, they referred to Moses who gave their fathers manna in the wilderness (John 6:30-31), but JESUS refuted this and told them that GOD, and not Moses, gave them the manna that sustained their ancestors in the wilderness (Exodus 16:11-16). However, before they asked, JESUS already pointed out their wrong motive for seeking HIM (John 6:26). JESUS warned them against making material gains the bases for seeking HIM, because of its temporary nature and not having eternal value. Many people who disregard GOD today, are asking for signs in terms of "what is in it for me?" If they cannot perceive this, they will not believe.

However, GOD created man, and through salvation, provided for man all the blessings and every good gift that pertains to life and godliness. This HE did for man long before anyone got saved, but they can only be spiritually discerned. The format, in which they exist, cannot be understood and received by the natural mind. The scriptures confirm, in the Book of Hebrews, that coming to GOD requires that one should believe HIS existence and the truth that HE rewards those who diligently seek HIM (Hebrews 11:6). GOD does not work with half-truths, hence it is not good enough to believe in the existence of GOD, if you are not willing to believe that HE rewards those who seek HIM with their whole heart (Jeremiah 29:13). The Greeks, on the other hand, seek wisdom in order to believe in GOD. This is evidenced in the reactions of some in Athens when Paul reasoned with the Jews and Gentiles concerning JESUS.

Acts 17:18 (NKJV)

"Then certain Epicurean and Stoic philosophers encountered him. And some said, 'What does this babbler want to say?' Others said, 'He seems to be a proclaimer of foreign gods,' because he preached to them Jesus and the resurrection."

Paul preached to them JESUS and the resurrection, and he was referred to as a babbler, because he did not make sense to all their five senses. They scheduled to hear Paul again, because they were never tired of acquiring new information and new doctrines that stimulated their five-sense-based reasoning. Thus, a combination of the Jews' and Greeks' philosophies of the truth make up the fleshly approach of viewing and responding to circumstances, situations and activities. These worldly perspectives can never be aligned with the spirit of GOD. To deny the existence of GOD in what they perceive with their five senses about the creation of the world (Romans 1:19-20) means denial to their minds, and blinds unbelievers to the light of gospel.

As a believer, to be an effective ambassador of the kingdom of GOD on earth, you must insist on your thoughts aligning with the word of GOD. It is the most effective way of resisting deception and all the different attacks of the enemy – both subtle and obvious. The word of GOD is the sword of the Spirit and it is life-giving and peace! It is JESUS's guaranteed strategy for success and victory for a spirit being. Thus, sticking to scriptures, as the foundation and source of our view of the world around us, is the key to successfully exercising our spiritual authority. It does not matter how much sense anything makes, a fleshly approach would yield absolutely nothing.

This is probably the most vicious tactic of the devil to disenfranchise GOD's children and deceive them into not taking GOD by HIS word. JESUS is the Way, the Truth and the Life (John 14:6), but many Christians come into the Way and get stuck at the door. They do not continue to the Truth, which is the word of GOD (John 17:17), so that they can know (become intimate with) the truth, in order to be equipped to live the abundant Life (John 17:2-3). Thus, JESUS is not fully beneficial to them; HE is only the Way for them, not the Truth, and not the Life. It is sad. However, as a person, you can make a decision today, and change that in your life.

At work, among your unbelieving family members and your friends, and anywhere else you may find yourself, remember that you are different and are supposed to think differently. Therefore, stop trying to fit in. Light and darkness have nothing in common (2 Corinthians 6:14-18). You must think differently and always be alert to recognize and to refute the lies of the enemy against you. I don't mean that you should challenge everyone you meet, who has a different world view from you. However, if you are required to do things that are a product of how the world thinks, then you must take a stand and be ready to defend the stand you take ("the hope that is in you").

You are different, so don't be afraid to defend your convictions or ashamed to stand for CHRIST. When you believed, you were separated unto GOD, because you are HIS. JESUS died for you so you can become HIS. 1 Corinthians 1:30 says that HE did not only give you redemption, and righteousness, but also sanctification. Sanctification means "set apart for something or someone." As a born-again Christian, you have been set apart for CHRIST. Therefore stop trying to fit in with the world. GOD loves you passionately (John 3:16; Romans 8:32; Ephesians 3:17-19), therefore, resolve to be proud of, and to identify with HIM always, regardless of who is involved (Matthew 10:33). Be reassured that if you stand firm for HIM, HE will defend you! Praise the LORD!

Be reassured that if you stand firm for HIM, HE will defend you!

CHAPTER 9

COMPARING NEW TESTAMENT BELIEVERS TO OLD TESTAMENT SAINTS

Matthew 11:11 (KJV)

"Verily I say unto you, among them that are born of women there hath not risen a greater than John the Baptist: notwithstanding he that is least in the kingdom of heaven is greater than he."

JESUS made a profound statement (in Matthew 11:11 above) which underlines the authority and power that born-again Christians inherited in CHRIST JESUS. None of all the Old Testament saints could compare to John the Baptist in authority, power, message, and in favor with GOD. That means that John the Baptist was greater than Adam and Eve (although these were not born by a woman, they disobeyed GOD), Abel, Enoch, Noah, Abraham, Lot, Moses, Samuel,

David, Elijah, Elisha, Isaiah, Jeremiah, Daniel, Nehemiah, Ezra and all the other prophets of the Old Testament. To get a full understanding of the extent of John's greatness, study the Old Testament for the great exploits done by the saints listed above, and others. Let's review a few of the exploits of some of these Old Testament saints, who, although they were great in their generations, were not as great as John the Baptist. What made John the Baptist greater than all these Old Testament saints?

In the summary of Enoch's life and relationship with GOD, the Bible says that he *"lived 365 years, walking in close fellowship with God. Then one day he disappeared, because God took him"* (Genesis 5:23-24, NLT). Enoch "walked" with GOD, to the point that he did not die, he just disappeared because the LORD took him. That's a wonderful testimony, yet John was greater than him. Verse 22 emphasizes the fact that Enoch, at the age of 65, had his first son, Methuselah, and then walked with GOD for additional 300 years, during which time he had other sons and daughters. Enoch enjoyed intimate relationship with GOD for about 365 years. Is it possible that he became so spiritual, living in close fellowship with GOD, that his material body dissolved and he disappeared? We know that he was a man of faith because he was featured on the "Faith's Hall of Fame" (Hebrews 11), as a person who pleased the LORD (Verse 5). Yet, John was greater than him.

Another example is Abraham. In Chapter 14 of Genesis, after an alliance of five kings led by Chedorlaomer, king of Elam, he fought and defeated the rebel kings of Sodom, Gomorrah, Admah, Zeboiim, and Bela (also called Zoar) as these used to be subject to Chedorlaomer's group. The victorious invaders then plundered Sodom and Gomorrah, taking with them all the spoils of war and the food supplies. They also captured Lot – Abram's nephew who lived in Sodom – and carried away all they could take (Genesis 14:8-20, NLT).

When Abram heard it, with his own 318 home-trained soldiers, "men who had been born into his household" (Verse 14), he went after these bully kings and recovered all they had taken in their conquest. The event that followed the great exploits of Abraham (verses 18-20) revealed that his conquest was because of his relationship with GOD. Abraham was greeted on his way back from the battle by a High Priest of GOD, Melchizedek, to whom he, Abraham, gave "a tenth of all the goods he had recovered" (Verse 20).

Abraham's faith extended his blessings to all the generations of the earth. He left his home and familiar territory to a strange land at the request of GOD (Genesis 12:1, Hebrews 11:8-10); he believed GOD to have a son at a very old age (Genesis 15:1-18; 21:2-3; Hebrews 11:11), which he did; and ultimately agreed to offer his only begotten son, Isaac, as a sacrifice to GOD (Genesis 22:1-12; Hebrews

11:17-19). Abraham exhibited the kind of faith that was placed in a category by itself, and yet John the Baptist was greater than him! John was referred to as being "more than a prophet" (Matthew 11:9 NLT), and not necessarily that he had more faith. In what way was John greater than Abraham?

The Bible also records the great exploits of Moses as the man that GOD used to keep HIS promise to Abraham that HE would deliver the children of Israel from the land of bondage. From the circumstances surrounding his birth – picked by the river bank and raised as the son of the Pharaoh's daughter – to his encounter with GOD at the burning bush that was not consumed, and where he received the instructions from GOD for the ultimate purpose of his life, Moses remained true to the calling upon his life.

Moses was called to deliver his people from Egypt, with the demonstration of the ten plagues that forced the king of Egypt to let them go. He was a great prophet and an awesome minister of GOD. GOD gave him an excellent character witness when HE rebuked Aaron and Miriam as they murmured against him, saying, *"My servant Moses... is faithful in all mine house"* (Numbers 12:7, KJV). GOD also differentiated between HIS relationship with Moses, from those of other prophets: while HE spoke in dreams, symbolism, types and shadows with other prophets (Verse 7), with Moses, HE spoke to him *"mouth to mouth, even apparently, and not in dark speeches"* (Verse 8). Yet, John was adjudged by JESUS to be greater than Moses.

Elijah and Elisha were two Old Testament prophets who were respected for doing great exploits through their relationships with GOD. Elisha was endowed with the "double portion" of the spirit of Elijah (2 Kings 2:9), just as Elijah prophesied (2 Kings 2:10).

The following miracles were associated with Elijah's ministry as a prophet in Israel:

1. Causing the rain to cease for three and a half years (1 Kings 17:1)

2. Being fed by the ravens (1 Kings 17:4)

3. Miracle of the barrel of meal and cruse of oil (1 Kings 17:14)

4. Resurrection of the widow's son (1 Kings 17:22)

5. Calling of fire from heaven on the altar (1 Kings 18:38)

6. Causing it to rain (1 Kings 18:45)

7. Prophecy that Ahab's sons would all be destroyed (1 Kings 21:22)

8. Prophecy that Jezebel would be eaten by dogs (1 Kings 21:23)

9. Prophecy that Ahaziah would die of his illness (2 Kings 1:4)

10. Calling fire from heaven upon a total of 102 soldiers (2 Kings 1:10-12)

11. Parting of the Jordan (2 Kings 2:8)

12. Elijah was also taken up to be with the LORD without dying; rather, he "went up by a whirlwind into heaven" (2 Kings 2:11).

Elijah was a great prophet, and going by the list of miracles above, he did great exploits in his ministry, but again, John the Baptist was greater than him.

Bible scholars believe that Elisha performed exactly twice the recorded miracles performed in Elijah's ministry (David Pyles, http://www.bcbsr.com/survey/eli.html).

The miracles associated with Elisha include:

1. Parting of the Jordan (2 Kings 2:14)

2. Healing of the waters (2 Kings 2:21)

3. Curse of the she bears (2 Kings 2:24)

4. Filling of the valley with water (2 Kings 3:17)

5. Deception of the Moabites with the valley of blood (2 Kings 3:22)

6. Miracle of the vessels of oil (2 Kings 4:4)

7. Prophecy that the Shunammite woman would have a son (2 Kings 4:16)

8. Resurrection of the Shunammite's son (2 Kings 4:34)

9. Healing of the gourds (2 Kings 4:41)

10. Miracle of the bread (2 Kings 4:43)

11. Healing of Naaman (2 Kings 5:14)

12. Perception of Gehazi's transgression (2 Kings 5:26)

13. Cursing Gehazi with leprosy (2 Kings 5:27)

14. Floating of the axe head (2 Kings 6:6)

15. Prophecy of the Syrian battle plans (2 Kings 6:9)

16. Vision of the chariots (2 Kings 6:17)

17. Smiting the Syrian army with blindness (2 Kings 6:18)

18. Restoring the sight of the Syrian army (2 Kings 6:20)

19. Prophecy of the end of the great famine (2 Kings 7:1)

20. Prophecy that the scoffing nobleman would see, but not partake of, the abundance (2 Kings 7:2)

21. Deception of the Syrians with the sound of chariots (2 Kings 7:6)

22. Prophecy of the seven-year famine (2 Kings 8:1)

23. Prophecy of Benhadad's untimely death (2 Kings 8:10)

24. Prophecy of Hazael's cruelty to Israel (2 Kings 8:12)

25. Prophecy that Jehu would smite the house of Ahab (2 Kings 9:7)

26. Prophecy that Joash would smite the Syrians at Aphek (2 Kings 13:17)

27. Prophecy that Joash would smite Syria thrice but not consume it (2 Kings 13:19)

28. Resurrection of the dead man touched by Elisha's bones (2 Kings 13:21)

Elisha's work and miracles as a prophet were quite impressive, but John was greater than him.

JESUS CHRIST said it: *"I tell you the truth, of all who have ever lived, none is greater than John the Baptist. Yet even the least person in the Kingdom of Heaven is greater than he is"* (Matthew 11:11, NLT)! As great as we've seen that John the Baptist was, the least person in the kingdom of GOD is greater than John. Praise the LORD! Why?

Andrew Wommack in his review of Matthew 11:12 reveals something that gives us a little insight into what JESUS meant by "greater than".

> *Matthew 11:12 (KJV)*
>
> *And from the days of John the Baptist until now the kingdom of heaven suffereth violence, and the violent take it by force.*

> *Matthew 11:12 (NLT)*
>
> *And from the time John the Baptist began preaching until now, the Kingdom of Heaven has been forcefully advancing, and violent people are attacking it.*

Based on the Greek word "biazo" which was interpreted as "suffereth," both this verse and "present" in Luke 16:16 (*Strong's Concordance*), which also means "to force, i.e. (reflexively) to crowd oneself (into), or (passively) to be seized" (ibid), agree with the NLT, which reads, "the Kingdom of Heaven has been forcefully advancing." Andrew concluded in the Note 2 on Matthew 11:12 of his Bible Commentary:

"The idea that Jesus was communicating in both of these passages was that before the time of John the Baptist, the only way to approach unto God was through the Old Testament laws and sacrifices. In Jesus' time, these had become cold and cumbersome rituals in which the hearts of the people were far from God (Matthew 15:3-9). When John the Baptist came in the power of the Spirit (2 Corinthians 3:6), preaching a turning away from sin (Matthew 3:8) and faith in the coming Messiah (Matthew 3:11), multitudes, who previously were not actively seeking God, began flocking to the wilderness to be baptized by John, confessing their sins and putting their faith in the coming Messiah. They were truly "pressing in" to the kingdom of heaven, overcoming any obstacle or opposition posed by laws, traditions, unbelief, or any power Satan threw at them, in order to receive the message that John preached. They were "violently resolved" in their zeal and forcefully pressing in to the kingdom of heaven."

Today, as in the days of John the Baptist, satan is opposing the preaching of the Gospel, and only those who are violently resolved to receive GOD's best, will have it (James 4:7).

According to Andrew's discussion of Matthew 11:12, the indwelling of the Spirit of GOD seems to be a major difference. "Before the time of John the Baptist, the only way to approach unto God was through the Old Testament laws and sacrifices… but John the Baptist came in the power of the Spirit" (2 Corinthians 3:6). He also inferred that the power of the HOLY SPIRIT seemed to have enabled John to turn more people away from sin and to righteousness, as he pointed them to CHRIST.

We know that John worked with the power of the Spirit of GOD, but the born-again son of GOD has a newly created spirit, which is infused with the Spirit of CHRIST and then sealed with the HOLY SPIRIT, who is permanently resident inside of him. The ultimate purpose of all the Old Testament people, events, prophecies and laws, were to "bring us to CHRIST". Thus, the New Testament believer, who is the permanent dwelling place of CHRIST, has to be superior to his precursors. It is the indwelling Spirit of CHRIST, WHO has made us superior and greater than John the Baptist and the Old Testament saints. It is HE WHO gave us access to spiritual authority and power, and greatly enhanced our potentials to take the kingdom of heaven by force. We are therefore adequately equipped to do the greater works of forcefully advancing the kingdom of GOD, by the spiritual authority and power of GOD that resides in us.

Think about what these Old Testament prophets were able to do without the indwelling presence of GOD, yet now, that power lives in us. This power is proportional to the power that raised CHRIST from the dead (Ephesians

1:19). These faith legends are among the crowd of witnesses (Hebrews 12:1) that have joined the angels to cheer us on to do more, with what we have in CHRIST JESUS.

Without specifically giving us the authority and power, I believe that we could still have been able to teach satan the manifold wisdom of GOD, just because of the indwelling Spirit of CHRIST in us; how much more, knowing that we have been given, not only the right to parade ourselves as sons of GOD, but to tread upon devils, and all satanic authority and power, in whatever format they assume.

My dear brothers and sisters, please rise and magnify GOD in your life, by taking charge against all the plans and purposes of the enemy against you. It does not matter how long they have been in operation, and it does not matter how they came; the truth is that if you resist them, bind them or cast them out and don't doubt, they will flee. It is a spiritual law! Rise from your dejection and start exercising your GOD-given authority over your circumstances, situations and all the demonic spirits that may have been bothering you; then watch your life change for good. Make this cloud of witnesses in Hebrews 12:1 proud, as you consciously ascend into living life from your born-again spirit, for better results!

CHAPTER 10

APPLICATIONS OF SPIRITUAL AUTHORITY

You are already blessed.

Palms 103:1-6 (KJV)

1 "Bless the LORD, O my soul: and all that is within me, bless his holy name.

2 Bless the LORD, O my soul, and forget not all his benefits:

3 Who forgives all thine iniquities; who heals all thy diseases;

4 Who redeemeth thy life from destruction; who crowneth thee with lovingkindness and tender mercies;

5 Who satisfieth thy mouth with good [things; so that] thy youth is renewed like the eagle's.

6 The LORD executeth righteousness and judgment for all that are oppressed."

Psalm 103 (as quoted above in Verses 3-6) has a list of some of the benefits of serving GOD, which have been made available to us in CHRIST. These benefits are supposed to be enjoyed on a regular basis by born again Christians, but that is not what is prevalent among believers.

1 Timothy 6:17 (KJV) declares that GOD gives us richly all things to enjoy, but many Christians are enduring all things in life. Some are neither enjoying Christianity nor their lives.

Let's take a look at what we should have in CHRIST:

- 1 Peter 2:24 says we were healed by the stripes of JESUS.

- Ephesians 1:3 says that we have been blessed with all spiritual blessings in heavenly places.

- Ephesians 1:6 says that we are highly favored (accepted).

- 2 Corinthians 8:9 says that we are meant to be rich by the poverty of CHRIST.

- Psalm 1:3 says we would prosper in whatsoever we do (that is according to HIS word).

- Many scriptures (including Mark 16:17) say that we have authority over satan to cast him out.

- Deuteronomy 28:3-13 (KJV) gives many more of our blessings

:

- 3 Blessed [shalt] thou [be] in the city, and blessed [shalt] thou [be] in the field. 4 Blessed [shall be] the fruit of thy body, and the fruit of thy ground, and the fruit of thy cattle, the increase of thy kine, and the flocks of thy sheep. 5 Blessed [shall be] thy basket and thy store. 6 Blessed [shalt] thou [be] when thou comest in, and blessed [shalt] thou [be] when thou goest out. 7 The LORD shall cause thine enemies that rise up against thee to be smitten before thy face: they shall come out against thee one way, and flee before thee seven ways. 8 The LORD shall command the blessing upon thee in thy storehouses, and in all that thou settest thine hand unto; and he shall bless thee in the land which the LORD thy God giveth thee. 9 The LORD shall establish thee an holy people unto HIMSELF, as he hath sworn unto thee, if thou shalt keep the commandments of the LORD thy God, and walk in his ways. 10 And all people of the earth shall see that thou art called by the name of the LORD; and they shall be afraid of thee. 11 And the LORD shall make thee plenteous in goods, in the fruit of thy body, and in the fruit of thy cattle, and in the fruit of thy ground, in the land which the LORD sware unto thy fathers to give thee. 12 The LORD shall open unto thee his good treasure, the heaven to give the rain unto thy land in his season, and to bless all the work of thine hand: and thou shalt lend unto many nations, and thou shalt not borrow. 13 And the LORD shall make thee the head, and not the tail; and thou shalt be above only, and thou shalt not be beneath; if that thou hearken unto the commandments of the LORD thy God, which I command thee this day, to observe and to do [them]: (Note: JESUS has fulfilled the requirements for these blessing on our behalf)

JESUS has fulfilled the requirements for these blessing on our behalf

Why Are We Not Enjoying These Blessings on a Regular Basis?

I can guarantee that GOD is not the one withholding these blessings from us, because HE has already given them to us in CHRIST JESUS. Some people, who experience defeat in the different areas listed above, just accept it and move on. Many Christians view these anomalies only from the human point of view and this does not give them the correct spiritual perspective. Ephesians 6:12 says that we are in a war; however, JESUS has already won this war for us.

In this final chapter, we will learn how we can arise and take back what is ours. Also, we will learn how to exercise our GOD-given spiritual authority, to appropriate for ourselves the "goodies" which belong to us as sons of GOD! Remember that you are a blessed son of GOD! That is the gospel truth! You have authority over all devils.

Based on applicable definitions of authority (e.g. Dictionary.com; *Webster 1828 Dictionary*) and the meaning of being born again as revealed in the Bible, I offer you this definition of spiritual authority:

Spiritual authority is the privilege or right to act on behalf of GOD and our LORD JESUS CHRIST to enforce obedience to the laws (Word) of GOD, on spirits that are subject to us as born-again Christians. Praise the Lord!

For example:

- You have authority and power over ALL devils (Luke 9:1)

- You have authority over ALL the power of the enemy (Luke 10:19).

- You have authority and power against unclean spirits (Mark 16:17).

- You have authority and power to cast out devils (Matthew 10:1; Mark 16:17),

- You have authority to enforce obedience on devils (Mark 16:17)

- You have authority to tread on serpents, scorpions,

and over all the power of the enemy (Luke 10:19).

- You have authority and power to cure diseases (Luke 10:1),

- You have authority to heal the sick (Mark 16:18),

- You have authority to heal all types of sicknesses and all types of diseases (Matthew 10:1).

- You have the authority and power to preach the Gospel (Matthew 28:18-20; Luke 9:2. Mark 16:15).

- You have authority and power to determine your circumstances and situations as the Lord guides you (Mark 11: 23-24).

- You have authority and power as a son of GOD to manifest the riches that JESUS exchanged for your poverty (2 Corinthians 8:9)

So, rise up and take what belongs to you in the name of JESUS. Firmly establish your reign, and nothing can stop you.

The power and authority you have in JESUS is closer to you than any man or woman of GOD that you may want to consult. The distance between you and the manifestation of your GOD-given power and authority is determined by what you believe. You will be far from that manifestation if you believe the wrong things, but intimately close to it if you believe correctly.

One of the many ways to exercise your authority is through self-awareness (Psalm 107:2). Self-awareness, here, means knowing who you are as a son of GOD. Scholars tell us that the first lesson in leadership is self-awareness. If you don't know who you are, then you cannot be a good leader. To understand the real you, and be aware of it so you can conduct yourself accordingly, you need to understand JESUS and the reason HE came on earth. Understanding JESUS, reveals who you are, and your assumed identity shapes your attitude, behaviors and actions, which in turn determine your effectiveness in exercising your spiritual authority. In the same way, understanding your place in CHRIST and seeing yourself as one with CHRIST influences your mindset about all possibilities, because all the power and authority in you will become obvious.

As a son of GOD, conducting yourself as one with authority and power is the first way to exhibit self-awareness of who you are. Thinking and acting as a son of GOD is key. If you don't conduct yourself as a son of GOD, satan will send his demons to treat you like a "punching bag." If you know that you have authority and power over satan and his lieutenants, you must conduct yourself accordingly. For example, you don't kneel down in order to bind and fight against satan and his demons. You command and order them out and expect them to obey you, because you are in charge. You have to acknowledge and walk in your inheritance in GOD.

If the word of GOD says you have authority and power, then you should gratefully acknowledge them (Philemon 1:6), and start using them. On a certain cool afternoon in 1993, when I was pregnant with my third child (my second daughter), as I was lying down, I sensed that someone had entered my room because I heard the door open and close. I turned to see who had entered the room because I was facing the wall. I didn't see anybody.

Then, I said, "It's only you, satan." Then, I turned back to my former position immediately, and slept off without thinking about it. My reaction was spontaneous and deliberate because I was confident that both satan and I knew that he could not touch me. I believe that I read that response from a book about how Smith Wigglesworth responded to satan; then I applied it and it worked.

What was more profound for me was the fact that in a church in Abuja, Nigeria, there was a young man whom satan had oppressed for over twenty years. He applied this same principle and it worked for him too. This means that GOD does not pick and choose who manifests HIS word; but men and women who have access to the same gospel, decide whether to believe GOD's word or not. Whosoever dares to believe and apply the word, gets GOD's purposed results, as implied in the word. Praise the LORD!

From a very young age, this young man had lived with a nightmare that woke him up at about 2 a.m. every night, with scratches all over his body. He was about thirty years of age when I visited his church in 2015. I gave the testimony during the first of a four-session, three-day meeting, that I had as a guest speaker in his church. Without coming out for prayers, he went home, determined to resist satan that night.

At the usual time, he was woken up as before, from his sleep, by the usual kind of nightmare; but instead of getting up to scream, casting and binding the devil, he quietly turned to his other side as he said the same words, "It is only you, satan." Shortly after, he slept, and to the best of my knowledge, those tormenting nightmares stopped, from that night.

He did not receive any prayers; he did not pray any extra prayers that night; he did not fast and pray; he only believed and acted on the fact that he had authority to resist satan and he would flee. That was exactly what happened! All Praise to JESUS.

To enforce obedience on satan, you, my brothers and sisters, must start by acknowledging the authority and power you've received from CHRIST, then assert yourself in spiritual things. Acknowledge means to believe, and say it out loud and boldly, that you have authority and power.

The first time I prayed for someone and the person got instantly healed, I actually had stepped out in faith. It was on the streets of Olodi Apapa, Lagos, Nigeria, when I first started early-morning street evangelism. This may have been my second week of going out early in the morning, at about 5-6 a.m., to preach. Standing at a street corner in front of a set of apartment buildings, and preaching on this particular day, I saw a woman with the corner of my right eye, dragging her oversized son behind her as she was crying and walking past, from behind me.

Suddenly, I stopped, and beckoned her to stop crying and take the boy back to her house, because the boy was healed. She immediately stopped and turned, without any hesitation and went back, as I turned and continued with my preaching. The woman had been pulling the boy to the taxi park, so she could find transportation to a hospital. The boy was about sixteen years old and much taller than his Mom. I later found out that he was so sick and weak that he couldn't stand on his legs, and his mother did not know what was wrong with him.

At about 12:00 noon the same day, my evangelism partner and I traced her back to her house. We were told that the boy was fine and had gone out playing soccer with his friends; he was completely healed. The woman told us that she had gone back to her house, laid him on his bed, and he had immediately slept the infirmaty off. When he woke up, he was completely healed. We praised the LORD and returned to our homes.

What I did was exercise my spiritual authority as I had read in the Bible. I did not hear a voice at that moment, telling me to call the woman. I did not see a vision prior to the time, that I was going to command a sick person to be healed and they would get instantly healed. None of that. The only thing was that I remembered that I had the authority and power to speak and it would happen. And you too, have that same authority! So, instead of being scared of bad dreams, for example, you can start by declaring what GOD says against such in Jeremiah 23:28-29.

The second part of 1 John 4:17 says that as CHRIST is, so are we in this world. So are we! But if you never acknowledge that this is who you are and start acting on it, then you would never experience it. However, if you would step out today and start exercising your authority, you too would start seeing results. Don't stop if nothing seems to happen the first few times. The word of GOD guarantees that you will see results if you don't give up.

Casting Out Devils

Concerning the casting out of devils, Christians have

to realize that they have the GOD-given right to cast them out, but the presence and activities of demons must be spiritually discerned (2 Corinthians 2:14-15). You must note that an adequate dose of the word of GOD has enough power in and of itself to cast out demons and reverse all demonic influence over anyone who believes (Psalms 107:20; Matthew 8:16; John 8:31-33, 15:3, and 17:17). The gospel is the power of GOD unto salvation ("sozo", which means forgiveness, deliverance, healing and prosperity).

A common question being asked by Christians is: Can a Christian be demonized? Here, I would like to refer to Andrew Wommack's Note 3 on Mark 1:37, where he opines that there are no distinctions between the oppressed, depressed, possessed, or any other form of influence of demons in the Bible, because all forms of the presence of the devil are dealt with, using the same dose of the power of GOD. Contrary to the belief of some Christians, a believer who does not "watch out" (1 Peter 5:8, NLT) and "put on the whole" of GOD's armory, can certainly be attacked and influenced by satan and his demons (Ephesians 6:12).

What should a Christian do, then? Realizing that he has authority over every power of satan, he should stand firmly in the name of JESUS, and cast him out. The devil would have no choice but to flee. Then the Christian in question should consciously build an intimate relationship with the LORD so that he can stay plugged into the source of that authority, otherwise, what happened to the seven sons of Sceva may be repeated in his life (Acts 19:13-17).

Another situation could be exercising authority over another person's will in casting devils out of them. If the person is not aware, you can cast out devils out of them, and follow up with giving them a good dose of the word of GOD after they've been delivered and are conscious. Because believers have authority over demonic spirits, but not over the will of other human beings, the person, who is aware that he is being demonized, must be willing and submit to be delivered from the devils' influence. He should also be open to believe and live by the Word of GOD; otherwise, the deliverance exercise will be futile or result in a reversed, worse situation for the individual, who would be invaded by more and worse demons than were previously cast out (Matthew 12:43-45). Remember, whether willing or not, and whether aware or not, you can forbid the demons from attacking you or affecting your circumstances and situations.

As mentioned above, the word of GOD, received, believed, and experienced, would make the demonized free indeed (John 8:32). They will be free from the present situation and free from further attacks and comebacks. Thus, all Christians have the authority over all the power and authority of evil spirits (Matthew 10:1 and Mark 16:17), and should use them as needed.

We also saw in 1 Samuel 16 where David, by playing instruments, which were supposed to be used to praise and worship GOD, helped King Saul whenever he was tormented by a demon.

1 Samuel 16:23 (KJV)

And it came to pass, when the [evil] spirit from God was upon Saul, that David took an harp, and played with his hand: so Saul was refreshed, and was well, and the evil spirit departed from him.

Praise and worship are also mentioned in Psalm 8:2, as tools for overcoming the enemy (Matthew 21:16). Form the habit of always praising and thanking GOD as weapons of warfare. It is beneficial to worship GOD in the church and your prayer closets; however, a deliberate effort to reverence, reference, and defer to GOD in all you do throughout the day are acts of worship that keep you plugged to HIM always.

Psalms 8:2 (KJV)

Out of the mouth of babes and sucklings hast thou ordained strength because of thine enemies, that thou mightest still the enemy and the avenger.

The NLT says that praising GOD is also a way of "silencing your enemies and all who oppose you" (Psalm 8:2, NLT). So, take advantage of it. Engaging in praising, and worshiping the LORD with "joyfulness and gladness of heart" ensures that you do not serve your enemies (Deuteronomy 28:47-48). Praising and worshiping GOD underscores the fundamental reason that Lucifer, the beautiful angel, became satan. He coveted GOD's throne so that he could be worshipped as GOD (Isaiah 14). So, praising and worshiping GOD is one direct way to resist satan and to cast him out (Matthew 4:9). Note that pride was what caused Satan's original sin, because he couldn't stand to see God worshiped (Matthew 8:2).

The major way a Christian can continually enjoy the flow of blessings in his life is to insist on living in the supernatural. He may accidentally drink deadly things or pick up venomous serpents, without being hurt (Mark 16:17-18). These are the extensions of the blessings of the authority and power of GOD that work for him.

While there was no biblical example of people drinking deadly things in the New Testament, we know about the water of Marah that was bitter, in Exodus 15, but was also sweetened by a tree that GOD showed them. There is also a case of Paul in the Island of Melita, when he was bitten by a venomous serpent in Acts 28:3-5, but did not get hurt, to the surprise of the Islanders.

These biblical examples also show that deliberately picking up dangerous animals like serpents or drinking deadly things, would constitute tempting GOD (Matthew

4:7; Luke 4:12), and are therefore not protected by the authority and power of GOD in the believer.

Apart from casting out devils, a Christian can also demonstrate the supernatural by the laying on of hands. Through this means, the power of GOD can be transmitted into the body of a sick person for his healing. It can also be used to transfer power on GOD's chosen vessel, for the work of the ministry. This was the usual way that church leaders were anointed for service in the house of GOD (1 Timothy 4:14; Hebrews 6:2).

GOD specifically gave us power and authority in many scriptures, but Luke 10:19 and Mark 16:17 are two of the most direct of the scriptures:

Luke 10:19 (KJV)

Behold, I give unto you power to tread on serpents and scorpions, and over all the power of the enemy: and nothing shall by any means hurt you.

Luke 10:19 (NLT)

Look, I have given you authority over all the power of the enemy, and you can walk among snakes and scorpions and crush them. Nothing will injure you.

There is a division of labor when it comes to our

protection from harm. GOD does not shy away from HIS responsibility towards us, as some atheists claim. HE created the universe so uniquely, that it is able to support and sustain the numerous lives in it, with numerous different living conditions. The evolutionists have proposed many godless explanation for the suitability of the earth for life. But we know better: GOD created the universe!

With the events of Genesis 3, which left human beings incapable of successfully managing their affairs, but working under the weight of satan's control (Ephesians 2:3), GOD gave anyone who believes in HIM the authority and power to overthrow all satan's power and authority.

Some believe and teach that satan cannot harm a believer, but that is not verifiable, biblically. JESUS healed a "daughter of Abraham" who was bound by satan for eighteen years (Luke 13:16). There are also scriptures that warn against satan's attack on people (2 Corinthians 2:11, 2 Timothy 2:26, and 1 Peter 5:8-9).

If you are born again and walk daily with GOD, in the consciousness of who you are, whose you are, and the power and authority you have, then satan and his demons can only attack, but CANNOT harm you. It is a spiritual law! Praise the LORD!

Physical laws tell us how physical and material things work and are usually expressed in science. For example, the law of gravity tells us that all material things obey the gravitational pull. Likewise, moral and spiritual laws tell us how human beings and spirit beings ought to behave, respectively, but don't always behave that way. The spiritual realm has laws that guarantee that superior beings have authority over the lower spirits, according to their rank.

Before you were born again, your spirit was dead (Genesis 2:17; 3:6), and therefore it became subject to satan (Romans 6:16, Ephesians 2:1-3). Then you believed in JESUS and GOD created a brand new spirit within your heart, infused it with the Spirit of CHRIST, sealed that union with HIS Spirit; and then you, the brand new spirit, got delivered from under satan's hold; and was translated to the right hand of GOD in the heavenly places, above all devils: *"Far above all principality, and power, and might, and dominion, and every name that is named, not only in this world, but also in that which is to come:"* (Ephesians 1:21).

This spiritual relocation implies higher authority and power over all other spirits below you. Praise the LORD! Although, the demon spirits may want to violate this law as they seek "whom they may devour" (1 Peter 5:9), you have the authority to force them to yield.

1 Peter 5:8-9 (KJV)

8 "Be sober, be vigilant; because your adversary the devil, as a roaring lion, walketh about, seeking whom he may devour:

9 Whom resist steadfast in the faith, knowing that the same afflictions are accomplished in your brethren that are in the world."

This book was written for this purpose. The goal is to help Christians understand some of these spiritual hierarchical schemas and their associated implications.

Unforgiveness is a Killer

2 Corinthians 2:10-11 (KJV)

10 "To whom ye forgive any thing, I [forgive] also: for if I forgave any thing, to whom I forgave [it], for your sakes [forgave I it] in the person of Christ;

11 Lest Satan should get an advantage of us: for we are not ignorant of his devices."

As a spirit being, when you harbor unforgiveness you open the door for the devil to come into your heart to cause untold harm. Paul associates unforgiveness with satan having the advantage over us, to wreak havoc, and suggests that we can inadvertently, by not forgiving, suffer all kinds of attacks from the enemy.

There is absolutely no reason to have special demon-casting or deliverance ministry, or get unhealthily focused on the devil and his agents, because he that is in you is greater than all the devils put together (1 John 4:4). However, equally spiritually unhealthy is being ignorant of the devices of satan. Peter says for us to be vigilantly watching against satan and his possible attacks (1 Peter 5:8).

Effectively dealing with the devil requires that we recognize that he exists, that his mission is to "kill, steal, and destroy" (John 10:10) and to know that we have the upper hand over him and his demons. Also, our advantage over him is enhanced by our acting promptly, whenever he surfaces. However, you cannot act promptly if you are not alert and ready to act.

If, on the other hand, you get scared, then satan has already taken the upper hand against you, because that fear is from the devil (2Timothy 1:7). For "GOD has not given us the spirit of fear, but of power and love and of sound mind."

GOD has not given us the spirit of fear, but of power and love and of sound mind.

Don't be overtly and excessively conscious of, or always casting out the devil; and in the same vein, don't act ignorantly of his mission and devices. However, being excessively focused on GOD, keeps you in perfect peace (Isaiah 26:3) and enables you not to give place to the devil (Ephesians 4:27), as well as not reducing your "strength" in the face of adversity (Proverbs 24:10)

Proverbs 24:10 (KJV)

[If] thou faint in the day of adversity, thy strength [is] small.

It might interest you to know that the presence of GOD and the presence of the devil are not mutually exclusive (Hebrews 13:5). This means that one does not necessarily go away because the other is with you. Remember the Spirit of CHRIST is always present with you, because HE is in you and you in HIM.

Hebrews 13:5 (KJV)

[Let your] conversation [be] without covetousness; [and be] content with such things as ye have: for he hath said, I will never leave thee, nor forsake thee.

Satan on the other hand is always *"your adversary the devil, as a roaring lion, walketh about, seeking whom he may devour:"* (1 Peter 5:8, KJV). The Bible does not say that when you are present with the LORD, satan takes a break; no, he does not; but arm yourself with the consciousness that he cannot touch you. So, you can go about your business, and be ready to act if the need arises. For example, I was in a hospital room with my third child, after an eventful child-birth. I had excessive bleeding, which caused me to die for a couple of hours. I was transferred to another hospital where I was confirmed dead. My husband took me back home and I came back to life as we arrived back at our apartment. Taking a nap the next afternoon alone with my new baby in my room, a man in a floral sunny shirt and shorts walked and stood by the door. I didn't hear him open the door, but there he was as I opened my eyes.

He looked at me and said, "You are alone."

Reflexively, without thinking, I said, "I am never alone, because CHRIST said he will never leave me nor forsake me." The man disappeared before I finished bragging about my faithful JESUS. Then I realized that my visitor was not human. Why was he there? To finish the job he had started the day before? I just thanked the LORD for HIS continued deliverance. Praise the LORD!

Understanding the devices, or the different strategies that the devil uses in his attacks, can be useful in effectively dealing with him. Being complacent with sin, holding unto offenses, and not believing, thinking, speaking and acting on the word GOD, can make a Christian an easy target of the devil (1 John 1:9 and Matthew 18:21-35).

Walking in forgiveness, like walking in love, is a decision. Both of them involve exercising your will to choose. This statement is not an attempt to minimize what and how you feel. The truth is that regardless of what happened or who hurt you, the only thing holding you back from where you are and the forgiveness you so badly need, is your perspective about what was done and who did it. Since there is nothing new under the sun (Ecclesiastics 1:9), it means that the same situation you found yourself, has happened to someone, somewhere, at a certain point, with the same or different outcomes. Proverbs 24:10 (KJV) says that if you "faint in the day of adversity," it is not the adversity that has overpowered you, but because your "strength [is] small," which means that the source of your inner resolution, faith, or source of energy is constrained (*Strong's Concordance*). It is less likely to submit to someone and overpower them in a contest. When you yield yourself to satan (Romans 6:16) by holding unto an offense, exercising your GOD given authority over him becomes difficult. Paul in admonishing Timothy on overcoming all forms of challenges said no one goes to battle cumbered with a heavy load (Hebrews 12:1; 2 Timothy 2:4).

2 Timothy 2:4 (TPT)

3 Overcome every form of evil[c] as a victorious soldier of Jesus the Anointed One. 4 For every soldier called to active duty must divorce himself from the distractions of this world so that he may fully satisfy the one who chose him.

5 An athlete who doesn't play by the rules will never receive the trophy, so remain faithful to God![d]

2 Timothy 2:3-5 (KJV)

*3 Thou therefore endure hardness, as a good soldier of Jesus Christ. 4 **No man that warreth***

> *entangleth himself with the affairs of [this] life; that he may please him who hath chosen him to be a soldier.*
>
> *5 And if a man also strive for masteries, [yet] is he not crowned, except he **strive lawfully**.*

Although Paul was not talking about offenses, in particular, unresolved conflicts and unforgiveness can constitute a significant barrier to disarm the devil and its demons effectively. JESUS said that offenses are inevitable, but "woe" unto or sorrow awaits anyone who offends (Matthew 18:7). Since we know that the author of all offenses is satan, a believer must choose not to give the devil a place by not forgiving the offender. Moreover, he should make an effort not to be the offender. It may not be possible to avoid all offenses, but you choose not to offend and not allow offenses to entrap you with satan. As the agent of all evil works, satan's goal is usually more than the original offense; he would want to get you, the offended, in the state of mind that could trap you in your circumstances, situations, and a web of activities he may have orchestrated. It would be best if you got rid of the offense faster than it would take sadness and depression to find a parking space in your mind.

As Word enforcement agents, you need to adopt the commitment and discipline of a soldier. In 2 Timothy 2: 3-6, Paul gave three leadership competencies that candidates for church leadership ought to acquire: be disciplined, the attitude of a soldier, adherence to the rule of engagement of an athlete. Being disciplined implies the commitment, diligence, and focus of the believer. The truth that believers have an enemy who is actively and relentlessly waging wars against us begs our discipline and continuous watchfulness.

The influence of satan to make you keep scores of wrongdoings is one of the most prevalent, but subtle double-edged attack strategies of the devil. For example, satan causes someone to offend you, influence you to take offense and resist forgiveness, then gains access into your affairs

As a soldier, you need to focus on the multiple-prongs benefits of forgiveness, staying committed to your cause, choosing to be sensitive to the Word of your COMMANDER IN CHIEF and not your feelings, and remembering that the associated hardships are temporary and sometimes inevitable.

fully to exacerbate strife and create all kinds of confusion (James 3:16). As a soldier, you need to focus on the multiple-prongs benefits of forgiveness, staying committed to your cause (1 Samuel 17:29), choosing to be sensitive to the Word of your COMMANDER IN CHIEF and not your feelings, and remembering that the associated hardships are temporary and sometimes inevitable (2 Corinthians4:16-18).

Also, be willing to stand your ground as if your life

depends on it; love your live not unto death (Revelation12:11), as a good soldier.

Since our wrestles with satan are ongoing (Ephesians 6:12), we must set ourselves to continuously beat him and maintain the victory JESUS gave us by acquiring an athlete's discipline. Satan is your inferior, and he wanders to and fro meddling in the affairs of this world as he looks for whom to devour (1 Peter 5:8). As a "Word enforcement officer," harboring unforgiveness is equivalent to being entangled with the affairs of this world (2 Timothy 2:4), and not contesting lawfully (2 Peter 2:5). Your commitment to your COMMANDER IN CHIEF, CHRIST, is for your safety and for maintaining victory. The enemy can penetrate your camp, whatever that is committed to your care, and wreck havoc in your life or the life of your loved ones. With the discipline of an athlete, who only wins with tenacity, focused mindset, and readiness by constant and consistent exercises, rise and take your position at your assigned post, traveling light without any offenses.

When you meditate on GOD's love and appreciate what it cost CHRIST to earn your forgiveness, you will be in a better position to make the decision to extend forgiveness to others. There is never a better time to forgive than now, because the earlier you do, the earlier you will shut the door to the lack of forgiveness that lays open the door for satan to come into your life. Also, doing the will of GOD requires that you obey GOD's word, which states that a "servant" of the LORD must not quarrel.

2 Timothy 2:24-26 (NLT)

24 "A servant of the Lord must not quarrel but must be kind to everyone, be able to teach, and be patient with difficult people.

25 Gently instruct those who oppose the truth. Perhaps God will change those people's hearts, and they will learn the truth.

26 Then they will come to their senses and escape from the devil's trap. For they have been held captive by him to do whatever he wants."

2 Timothy 2:24-26 (KJV)

24 And the servant of the Lord must not strive; but be gentle unto all [men], apt to teach, patient,

25 In meekness instructing those that oppose themselves; if God peradventure will give them repentance to the acknowledging of the truth;

26 And [that] they may recover themselves out of the snare of the devil, who are taken captive by him at his will.

There is no doubt that there are still demons and demon-possessed individuals today. In fact, Ephesians 2:2 is explicit in saying that all those who live in disobedience to GOD today are subject to demonic influence.

Ephesians 2:2 (NLT)

"You used to live in sin, just like the rest of the world, obeying the devil--the commander of the powers in the unseen world. He is the spirit at work in the hearts of those who refuse to obey God."

It is therefore pertinent that every child of GOD should understand the spiritual undercurrents of the Christian life and walk successfully, exercising his authority and maintaining the sanctity of the spirit.

CONCLUSION

GOD has given us "all things to enjoy" (I Timothy 6:17), but most Christians misinterpret that to mean GOD has given us all things to endure. As a result, many Saints miss GOD's blessings. It is tragic for any one of HIS children to continue to live defeated lives or die prematurely. It is not HIS will for us to be poor, deprived of blessing, depressed, or discouraged because of the GOD-given authority with the resurrection power.

I Timothy 6:17 (The Passion Translation), "Charge them that are rich in this world, that they be not high-minded, nor trust in uncertain riches, but in the living God, who giveth us richly **all things to enjoy.**"

> *17 To all the rich of this world, I command you not to be wrapped in thoughts of pride over your prosperity, or rely on your wealth, for your riches are unreliable and nothing compared to the living God. **Trust instead in the ONE who has lavished upon us all good things, fulfilling our every need.***

If you read this text until these Biblical principles become active in your life, you will begin walking in the victory GOD gave in CHRIST JESUS. GOD, CHRIST, the HOLY SPIRIT, and the angels are always working with you; they are for you and never are against you!

Spiritual Authority: Victory for Everyday Living reveals who you are in CHRIST JESUS in ways that you could never imagine!

Spiritual Authority: Victory for Everyday Living exists to provide additional insight into the spiritual components of a born-again Christian and expound on why our GOD-given spiritual authority is critical in maintaining the victory JESUS paid a high price to give us.

The reality about Christianity eludes many Christians and I believe that is why the world does not feel the effects and benefits of the birth, death and resurrection of our LORD JESUS CHRIST! Furthermore, this book exists to open your eyes to the realities of your new nature as a Christian: the supernatural authority and power you have to effectively manage your circumstances, situations and the activities of the demonic world. You also are able to appreciate the unprecedented honor and privilege you have in CHRIST JESUS.

Do not expect to become an expert in exercising your authority overnight. The journey of a million miles begins with the first step of "becoming aware of where you are going and the direction", and I believe that this book will be a great guide.

I hope *Spiritual Authority: Victory for Everyday Liv-*

Conclusion

ing fills any gaps between what you may already know about our spiritual authority and where many Christians are in their understanding of a believer's spiritual realities.

I hope this book connected you to the reality of who you are (Spirit, Soul, and Body), and continuously reminds and confirms the rights you have as a born-again believer.

APPENDIX

A

Biography

Dr. Ifeoma Okechukwu has been a licensed and ordained minister of GOD since 2006. A former atheist who encountered the LORD and got saved on February 8, 1986. Ifeoma's ministry began in Nigeria, where she was the Cell Leader of a women's home fellowship. She immigrated to the United States in 1995 where GOD opened avenues for her to minister.

She served as an Associate Pastor of the Second Olivet Baptist Church in Detroit, Michigan, from 2014-2018, then joined and became a Bible Teacher at the House on the Rock Church in Ypsilanti. She is also the Founder of Favoured Beulah Ministry, Nigeria, Inc., and Favoured Beulah International, USA, Inc., non-profit organizations committed to helping widows and their children realize their life goals. As a Christian missionary, Ifeoma travels yearly to different parts of Africa and the Caribbean to preach the gospel of our LORD JESUS CHRIST. From 2007 till date, Ifeoma has hosted different radio programs: "The Gospel Truth" and "Arise and Shine" both in Nigeria and the USA respectively.

Apart from holding a Master's degree in Mathematics

and a PhD in Engineering, Ifeoma also obtained the Word of Faith International Christian Center Bible College diploma in 2004. Ifeoma Okechukwu is a wife, mother of five children, and a career woman who resides in Detroit, Michigan.

Ifeoma is passionate about sharing her faith with unbelievers as well as helping believers learn how to maximize their potentials in CHRIST JESUS.

Spiritual Authority Fundamentals was born out many years of walking with GOD.

B

Abbreviation:

1. NKJV: New King James Version
2. KJV: King James Version
3. NLT: New Living Translation
4. TPT: The Passion Translation
5. MSG: The Message Bible

C

References

1. Baker, 1992; Losing Faith in Faith: From Preacher to Atheist Paperback; Publishers: Freedom From Religion Foundation Inc. Madison WI, USA

2. Copeland, 2001; You Are The Prophet of Your Life; Publications: Kenneth Copeland Publications

3. Elijah's ministry (David Pyles, http://www.bcbsr. com/survey/eli.html).

4. Evans, 2019; https://www.youtube.com/watch?v=-JqRTghk_f2Q

5. Hagin. K. E. (2001); *The Believer's Authority;* FAITH LIBRARY PUBLICATIONS

6. Heritage Foundation: https://www.americanheritage.com/race-cleansing-america

7. Lewis, 1952; *Mere Christianity: Description: Publisher: Geoffrey Bles*

8. Phillips, J. B. (1995). *New Testament in Modern English.* Simon and Schuster.

9. Pope Benedict XVI (Vatican City, Nov 14, 2012 / 10:45 am): https://www.catholicnewsagency.com/news/practical-atheism-more-destructive-than-disbelief-pope-says

10. *Strong's Concordance*

11. Tozer, 2015; The Pursuit of God (Updated, Annotated):Publisher: Aneko Press

12. *Wommack, 2011; One Year with JESUS Devotion-*

al. Andrew Wommack App

13. Wommack, 2005; *Spirit, Soul and Body*, Published by Andrew Wommack Ministries, Inc.

14. Wommack, 2012; Bible Living Commentary Software

CPSIA information can be obtained
at www.ICGtesting.com
Printed in the USA
BVHW041700080721
611459BV00015B/923